THE ALCHEMY
STONES

De cavernis metallorum occultus est, qui Lapis est venerabilis. HERMES

THE ALCHEMY
S·T·O·N·E·S

*Use the Wisdom of the Ancient Alchemists
to Transform Your Life*

M. E. WARLICK

Marlowe & Company
New York

◄◐►

For Meme, Cleo and Callie

THE ALCHEMY STONES: *Use the Wisdom of the Ancient Alchemists to Transform Your Life*

Text copyright © M.E. Warlick 1997
Illustrations of alchemy stones copyright © Richard Earley 1997
This edition copyright © Eddison Sadd Editions 2002

The right of M.E. Warlick to be identified as the author of this work has been asserted by her in
accordance with the Copyright, Designs and Patents Act 1988.

Published in the United States by Marlowe & Company
An Imprint of Avalon Publishing Group Incorporated
161 William Street, Sixteenth Floor
New York, NY 10038

First published in the United States in 1997 as *The Philosopher's Stones* by Tuttle Publishing, New York

AN EDDISON • SADD EDITION
Edited, designed and produced by
Eddison Sadd Editions Limited
St Chad's House, 148 King's Cross Road
London WC1X 9DH

All rights reserved. No part of this book may be reproduced in whole or in part without written
permission from the publisher, except by reviewers who may quote brief excerpts in connection with a
review in a newspaper, magazine or electronic publication; nor may any part of this book be reproduced,
stored in a retrieval system, or transmitted in any form or by any means electronic, mechanical,
photocopying, recording, or other, without written permission from the publisher.

Library of Congress Cataloging-in-Publication data is available.

ISBN 1-56924-569-X

9 7 5 3 1 2 4 6 8

Designed by Sarah Howerd

Phototypeset in Poliphilus MT and Blado MT italic using QuarkXPress on Apple Macintosh
Origination by Hung Hing Offset Printing Co. Ltd.
Manufactured in China

Distributed by Publishers Group West

FRONTISPIECE *In spring, the search begins in the earth and leads to the heavens.*
Alchemical symbols for the Sun and Moon, the King and Queen, Philosophic Sulphur
and Philosophic Mercury are all found in this landscape.

Contents

– INTRODUCTION –

ALCHEMY FOR PERSONAL TRANSFORMATION 7

– PART ONE –

YOUR ALCHEMY STONES 17

– PART TWO –

YOUR LABORATORY PROCEDURES 79

KEY TO THE ALCHEMY STONES 94

FURTHER READING 96

ACKNOWLEDGEMENTS 96

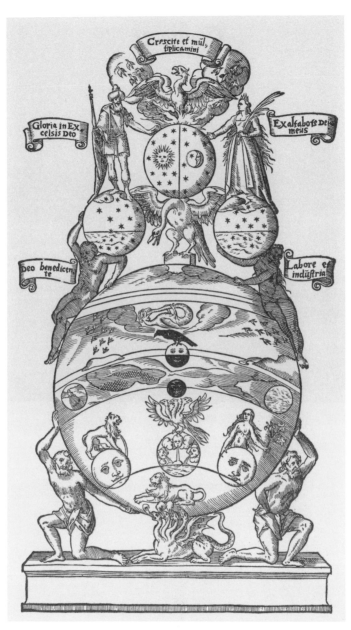

Alchemical operations are symbolized by birds and animals. The lion, crow, swan and phoenix represent stages of the work; the King and Queen, Sun and Moon are its goal.

– INTRODUCTION –

ALCHEMY FOR PERSONAL TRANSFORMATION

What is Alchemy?

EVERYONE loves a good mystery, and some of us are drawn particularly to mysteries of the past with their ancient wisdom steeped in myths, legends and symbols. Mythology, astrology, the tarot, runes and I-Ching have all experienced revivals in recent years, enjoyed by new generations who are interpreting their messages in fresh, innovative ways. Yet alchemy, one of the most enduring paths of spiritual knowledge, still remains an enigma to many. Vaguely known as the art of turning lead into gold, few people realize that a vast philosophy underlies this early science. Stretching back to ancient Egypt and classical Greece, alchemy has called and enticed people across the ages to decipher its mysteries.

As an art historian, my own interest has grown from an investigation of alchemical images and their influence on visual artists, from the surrealists in the early twentieth century down to the present day. Many of these artists have understood alchemy as a metaphor for the transformation that occurs in their studios, a symbolic model for turning raw materials into works of art. I began my own study by looking at general books on alchemy to understand the basic principles of its symbolic illustrations. Gradually my investigation has expanded to the earlier texts, manuscripts and printed books, appearing from the Middle Ages onward. This has been a most rewarding process for me, although I often feel, even after twenty years, that the journey is just beginning. Anyone starting a study of alchemy will be immediately challenged by its complicated terms and seemingly confusing descriptions of substances and operations. This is not to say that your study would necessarily be frustrating and discouraging. Rather, you will find that unravelling the puzzles of alchemy is a process that continues to grow and expand, offering deeper understanding, awareness and connections to your everyday life.

For me, over the years, alchemy and its symbols have evolved into a personal philosophy that I use to interpret signs found in daily life. In writing this book, I hope to share that process with you. For many of you, it will be an entertaining tool to help answer personal questions and guide your decisions. For others, this book may begin a wider study of alchemy and its philosophy. Wherever this book leads you, trust that alchemy is both old and timeless, and that it has a profound potential to change your life. This fountain of ancient wisdom has nourished seekers of spiritual enlightenment throughout the ages.

THE PURSUIT OF KNOWLEDGE

Alchemy is a quest for physical, mental and spiritual transformation. Evolving in both Western and Eastern cultures, this ancient art developed basic laboratory procedures to refine and purify metals. These operations became the foundation on which the modern sciences of biology, chemistry and physics have been built. The perceptive student of alchemy realizes, however, that these laboratory processes of transformation veil a deeper philosophy leading to self-knowledge, spiritual evolution and personal enlightenment.

What draws a person to alchemy? History tells many legends of alchemists magically led on to this mystical path. One story from the late Middle Ages concerns the Parisian alchemist, Nicolas Flamel, who dreamed one night of a beautiful manuscript. Soon afterwards, he found a manuscript like the one in his dreams, filled with strange symbols and authored by a mysterious 'Abraham the Jew'. Frustrated in his attempts to decipher the symbols, Flamel took a pilgrimage to the shrine of Saint Jacques de Compostela in northern Spain to seek help from the scholarly community there. A doctor named Master Canches was filled with astonishment and joy on seeing the manuscript, and he instructed Flamel on ways to unlock its secrets. Canches died soon afterwards, so Flamel returned alone to France where, aided by his wife Pérenelle, he was later able to transform mercury into both silver and gold. Flamel's story contains an important key to the alchemical pursuit. While dreams, chance or some twist of fate might initiate your interest in alchemy, only a dedicated search for knowledge and understanding, combined with a diligent application of what you have learned, will bring you wisdom and completion.

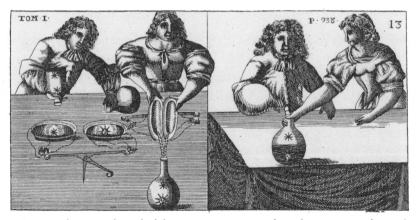

A man and woman share the laboratory operations. Balance between masculine and feminine principles is essential to perfect the Sun and Moon.

UNLOCKING THE SECRETS

Alchemical manuscripts, like the one found by Flamel, are filled with puzzling descriptions and mysterious symbols that represent the various substances and processes. These texts and their illustrations are difficult to decipher, intended as puzzles to discourage the unworthy from unlocking their secrets. Alchemy is a process that requires thought, reflection and proper action. As you begin to understand its physical operations, the deeper philosophical and spiritual mysteries will unfold.

The alchemist progresses in this quest through trial and error, learning from successes and failures alike. It is a spiralling process, in which you often return to where you have been before, but armed with past experiences and ready to attempt old challenges in a new way. A central alchemical axiom is *Solve et Coagula*, 'dissolve and coagulate'. With this constant repetition of separation and reunion, of letting go and gathering in, the work proceeds. The substances in the vessel fluctuate between fixed and volatile states, alternately solid and fluid, while the gases and liquids produced during the operations are continually evaporating and condensing. Simply put, alchemy is a process of persistent work and constant change that leads to the purification and refinement of the body, mind and soul.

Another central axiom of alchemy is *As above, so below*. The Earth and its creatures directly reflect the workings of the Universe ~ for the microcosm and the macrocosm are one. For this reason, alchemy is related closely to astrology. The Sun and the Moon are its two central characters, representing the masculine and feminine poles of being. The ancients thought that the Sun (gold) and the Moon (silver) were planets. These two, and

Beneath an arc of zodiac signs from Aries to Pisces, four women represent the Sun's significant passages, the solstices and equinoxes, which are crucial times for the alchemical work.

[9]

the remaining five planets, rule over the seven metals in their progression from lead to gold ~ Saturn (lead), Jupiter (tin), Mars (iron), Venus (copper) and Mercury (quicksilver). Alchemical operations are performed at designated times of the year, during appropriate astrological signs which guide proper operations in the laboratory.

The complexity of alchemical symbolism is often a challenge to the beginner, or Initiate, as you now are. A single substance can have several symbols: such as Primal Matter, the chaotic substance found at the beginning of the work, which is represented by both serpents and frogs. Conversely, a single symbol may carry multiple meanings: for example, a lion can represent the fixed masculine aspects of Primal Matter as well as the element Earth. Primal Matter and Earth are symbolically related, and so serpents, frogs and lions have similar meanings when they appear in alchemical imagery. Even though this symbolism may seem indecipherable in the beginning, it does have its own internal logic which will become apparent in time.

As with the Yin~Yang oppositions of Eastern philosophy, sexual duality and balance are central to alchemical lore. The King and Queen, the human symbols for the Sun and the Moon, represent the two opposing properties of Primal Matter: Philosophic Sulphur and Philosophic Mercury. During the alchemical operations, they are united, destroyed, separated, purified and then rejoined. The King, the Sun and gold are all 'masculine' aspects that complement their 'feminine' opposites: the Queen, the Moon and silver. The figures in the illustrations are not meant to represent real men and women, but rather they

The King and Queen unite as an Androgyne rising from the dragon of Primal Matter. A sunny tree signals their

perfection, while a bird feeding her chicks suggests the ability of the Philosopher's Stone to multiply its power.

symbolize dynamic properties of all matter. The masculine realm is active, hot, dry and fixed; the feminine is receptive, cool, moist and volatile. Throughout the alchemical operations, the masculine and feminine spheres exert their influence alternately on each other.

At the end of the work, the King and Queen fuse into a single perfect being ~ the Androgyne ~ a symbol of a harmonic balance between masculine and feminine poles. Whether you interpret these characters as dual aspects of your own personality, or as the dynamics of your relationships with others, you will find the battles, reconciliations and passionate love between the King and Queen can be useful models for personal growth.

To update alchemy as a tool for contemporary times presents some challenges. Its truths are universal, but its philosophy and imagery developed in earlier periods, when more polarized gender roles were the norm. However, in traditional alchemy, both 'masculine' and 'feminine' elements play essential roles throughout the work, and this balance can find a useful expression today when greater equality between the sexes is desired and sought. While this book preserves the essentials of alchemical philosophy, some of its messages have been reinterpreted for the contemporary reader.

PRACTISING ALCHEMY IN YOUR LIFE

Alchemy seeks to find the correspondences between matter and spirit, between body and soul. Hence, the key to the alchemical quest lies in the real world. Whatever you discover in these pages, seek new personal ways to apply its wisdom within your own life. Using its metaphors of nature, a rainy day becomes an opportunity for rest, solitude and recuperation. A brisk wind rustling through the leaves is a reminder of the potential for mental transformation. Seeing a black bird can remind you to let go of some troubling problem. Learn that life's disappointments can herald a time of transformation, renewal and personal growth. Death is an inevitable part of any cycle, but it is also the first phase of the alchemical process: as plants die, their seeds rest deep in the Earth and, after a gentle rain, they germinate, grow and eventually bear new fruit. Likewise, the alchemist must destroy Primal Matter and cleanse it of all its impurities before silver and gold are formed and the Philosopher's Stone appears, containing new potential for effortless growth and expansion.

Each season of the year brings a message for renewal. The hope and rebirth of spring, the abundance of summer, the harvest and transition of autumn and the cosy hibernation of winter, all complete the spiral of life in which we are all dancing. When you take the alchemical path, you will begin to see how closely the rhythms of your life parallel those of nature. Observe and interpret these natural signs that mark your progress to higher physical, mental and spiritual states.

The History of Alchemy

ALCHEMY is thought by many to have originated in Egypt as a spiritual ritual connected to early experiments in metallurgy. The legendary Egyptian philosopher, Hermes Trismegistus, the 'thrice-great Hermes', is one of the oldest and most important alchemical philosophers. Related to both the Egyptian god, Thoth, and to the Greek god, Hermes, this legendary figure was a man of many talents. Shown opposite, he points to the Sun and Moon ~ *As above, so below*. Of his many mystical writings, *The Emerald Tablet*, also shown opposite, is by far the most famous summary of alchemical wisdom. Many legends recount how Alexander the Great discovered these words in the great philosopher's tomb inscribed on a tablet of emerald, while others claim that Sarah, the biblical wife of Abraham, found them there.

Although the real author of this work may never be identified, its words reveal many of the basic tenets of alchemical symbolism and process. Medieval Latin and Arabic translations of this document derive from earlier, lost Greek and Syriac texts. The version shown here has been adapted from several modern translations. This is the basic philosophy of alchemy as a true spiritual path. It reveals the unity of all matter, as the microcosm of the Earth and the macrocosm of the heavens mirror and reflect each other. The Sun and Moon are parents of all things nurtured on Earth. Within the laboratory, through diligent efforts, the alchemist must separate this essence from impurities through a gentle but powerful process. As gases rise and fall in the vessel, a new, perfect substance is formed.

FROM ANCIENT EGYPT TO THE NEW WORLD

Transmitted to the Greeks from the Egyptians, alchemical lore adopted the classical view of the Universe, which placed the Earth at the centre of the cosmos and divided all matter into four elements ~ Earth, Water, Fire and Air. Although it differed from its Western counterpart, alchemy is also an ancient Chinese art. Eastern practitioners used five basic elements instead of four ~ Wood, Fire, Earth, Metal and Water ~ and they sought to produce a magic elixir that would bestow eternal life.

During the early Middle Ages, Jewish and Arabian alchemists introduced new laboratory procedures, expanding on the types of alchemical vessels, operations and applications. By the late Middle Ages, alchemy was practised commonly to produce medicines, tinctures, perfumes and other substances, in addition to the more ambitious quest of turning lead into gold. Throughout this period, alchemical teachings grew gradually through the writings of late classical, Islamic and medieval authors. During this era, when Christianity reigned in western Europe, alchemical philosophy was generally in harmony

THE

Emerald Tablet

of Hermes Trismegistus

*True it is, without falsehood, certain and most true. That which is above is like that
which is below, and that which is below is like that which is above,
to accomplish the miracles of One thing.
And as all things were made by One, so all things arose from this One by adaptation.
The father is the Sun, the mother the Moon.
The Wind carried it in its womb, the Earth is its nurse.
It is the father of all works of wonder throughout the whole world.
Its power is perfect.
If it is cast to Earth, it will separate the element of Earth from that of Fire,
the subtle from the gross.
With great sagacity it ascends gently from Earth to Heaven.
Again it descends to Earth, and unites in itself the power from things superior and inferior.
Thus you will possess the glory of the brightness of the whole world,
and all obscurity will fly far from you.
This thing is the strong fortitude of all strength, for it overcomes every subtle thing
and penetrates every solid substance.
Thus was the world created.
In this manner marvellous adaptations will be achieved.
For this reason I am called Hermes Trismegistus, because I hold three parts of
the wisdom of the whole world.
What I had to say about the operation of the Sun is completed.*

(Based on various translations compiled by Jon Marshall)

with the teachings of the Catholic Church. Alchemists often used religious metaphors, along with astrological symbols, to explain their processes ~ drawing on the lives of Adam and Eve, and Christ and the Virgin Mary, as spiritual parallels to the operations in the laboratory.

As the knowledge of alchemy spread, it came to be practised not only by dedicated philosophers, but also by charlatans, or 'Puffers', as they were known, who wanted to 'get rich quick'. During the Renaissance, the serious study of ancient texts returned and flourished throughout Europe. Hermetic scholars fought to purge alchemy of its foolish practitioners and to restore it to its elevated path of spiritual enlightenment.

Alchemy's two central characters, the King and the Queen, originated in the feudal structure of the Middle Ages. Later, with the Renaissance's fascination with classical Greece and Rome, mythological legends began to augment the existing Christian and feudal images. Classical gods and goddesses represented the seven ancient planets and metals, further enriching alchemy's visual tradition with elaborate and enigmatic illustrations.

The authors and illustrators of the manuscripts and printed books were always eclectic, gathering and transforming words and images to serve as secret symbols for their chemicals and processes. Through careful study and persistence, the dedicated Initiate identifies the substances needed for the work and reconstructs the order of the laboratory procedures. This is a challenging task, requiring constant vigilance and a lifetime's dedication. Only a few notable alchemists ever attained monetary success, although many undoubtedly recognized the fruitfulness of engaging in the work.

Alchemical images are rich with metaphors. The alchemist tends the vessel as a pregnant woman nurtures her unborn child. The substance must be cooked and watched like pots simmering gently over a fire.

Perhaps the failures of the many 'Puffers' gave alchemy its reputation as a vain and foolish quest for gold. By the seventeenth century, the alchemist had become a well-known symbol for human folly. Artists frequently depicted the impoverished alchemist working feverishly in a ramshackle laboratory, surrounded by manuscripts and equipment, oblivious to the surrounding chaos. During this same period, however, many new alchemical books were printed and embellished with complex illustrations, further expanding the wealth of its symbolism. Most of the illustrations in this book date from this period.

The Age of Enlightenment brought the first explorations of modern science which adopted the alchemists' laboratory operations and skills of observation. Although contemporary scientists and philosophers redirected the course of science, placing more emphasis on reason and empirical evidence, great thinkers like Sir Isaac Newton and Goethe continued to study alchemy and its philosophy. The Industrial Revolution created an even greater distance between modern experience and ancient hermetic wisdom. Yet, in spite of the materialism that apparently had seized control of both Europe and America, many ancient traditions continued to flourish underground.

A MODERN REVIVAL

In the late nineteenth century, the occult revival rekindled many ancient paths of spiritual wisdom, including alchemy. Hoping to share those mysteries with the modern world, writers, artists and scientists began to re-evaluate the alchemical tradition and discover anew its timely message. In the twentieth century, psychoanalysts, like Herbert Silberer and Carl Jung, used alchemy as a model for human psychological development. While this application may seem to be a modern reinterpretation, personal transformation has been a part of traditional alchemical philosophy since its earliest days. Hidden among the puzzling descriptions in old manuscripts is the continuing thread of alchemy's higher spiritual purpose. The creation of gold is secondary to the quest for self-knowledge and self-perfection that begins as the alchemist engages in the work. The more one grapples with the alchemical process, with its inevitable triumphs and disappointments, the more one comes to understand the Self. Primal Matter, the Philosopher's Stone and the alchemist are one.

The alchemist within a cauldron holds a symbol of Primal Matter.

When we begin to work with alchemy, we begin to change ourselves.

[15]

The alchemist stands on the double lion of Primal Matter, flanked by masculine and feminine symbols of the work. Above, the heavens influence the operations symbolized by the crow, the swan, the dragon, the pelican and the phoenix.

— PART ONE —

YOUR ALCHEMY STONES

FEW PEOPLE WHO STUDY ALCHEMY EVER EQUIP A LABORATORY WITH FLASKS and furnaces, although traditional alchemists certainly practise today. The twenty-eight alchemy stones included in this pack have been designed to give you some insight into the laboratory and its operations. Twenty-eight is a powerful number, being the sum of the seven sacred numbers, one to seven. This magic number is in harmony with the Moon's cycle, thus closely linked to our daily experience of the cosmos.

About the Stones

THE twenty-eight alchemy stones are divided into six groups, each of which is outlined below: alchemists, ingredients and tools, elements, planets and metals, stages of completion, and culmination. The shape of the stones is based on the rounded interior of the alchemist's flask. This vessel is also known as the 'Philosophic Egg'. The alchemist, like a mother hen warming her eggs, must gently heat and carefully observe the contents of the vessel throughout the work. Likewise, as you handle these tactile objects, your physical contact will heighten the resonance between you and their meanings. Each alchemy stone carries a traditional symbol to represent stages and components of the work, and their meanings are described individually in The Interpretations (*see pages 21~77*). These symbols appear within the stones just as the signs of the work appear to the alchemist within the vessel. Do not be surprised if, over time, the stones develop new and very personal meanings for you, clarifying and expanding those explanations provided here.

ALCHEMISTS

Within the alchemy stones there are three types of alchemists: Puffer, Initiate and Adept. Manuscripts warn of those who begin on the alchemical path with misguided intentions to acquire an easy fortune. These Puffers receive their name from the bellows that heat the fire in the alchemical furnace. Their vain pursuit of gold will end only in frustration if they remain oblivious to the spiritual aspects of alchemy. The Initiate, on the other hand, is an apprentice who begins to identify and seek the proper alchemical substances and processes. Finally, the Adept is one who has attained a significant level of achievement, while realizing that the process is cyclic and continually evolving.

INGREDIENTS AND TOOLS

The ingredients and tools include Primal Matter, Philosophic Sulphur, Philosophic Mercury, Salt, the Alembic and the Athanor. Primal Matter is the basic raw material, a unified single substance, comprising all that is necessary for the work to proceed. It contains two polarized properties ~ the masculine Philosophic Sulphur and the feminine Philosophic Mercury ~ which eventually will be refined into gold and silver. They are represented by the King and Queen and by the Sun and the Moon. A third ingredient, Salt, often represented by the god Mercury, is the necessary catalyst for joining the two opposing properties together.

The alchemical operations take place in the Alembic, a transparent glass vessel through which the alchemist can watch the various transformations. This vessel is contained within the Athanor, a furnace whose temperature the alchemist carefully controls in order to bring about fusion and perfection.

ELEMENTS

Primal Matter is composed of the four elements, held in suspension by a fifth, ethereal substance, called the Quintessence. These elements are Earth, Water, Fire and Air, and all matter contains them in differing proportions. They are also understood to represent states of matter: the Earth is solid, fixed, cold and dry; Water is liquid, volatile, cold and moist; Fire is gaseous, fixed, hot and dry; Air is gaseous, volatile, hot and moist.

ABOVE LEFT *The alchemist enters the laboratory with the lion and serpent of Primal Matter. He points to a symbol for Mercury which also must be present at the beginning.*
ABOVE RIGHT *A philosopher ponders the mysteries. The cube represents the stability of the four elements. Two birds in glass Alembics show the separation of the two principles.*

PLANETS AND METALS

The seven ancient planets are each connected to specific operations and stages in the alchemical work, and certain tasks are performed at prescribed astrological times during the year. The planets also rule over the seven metals as follows: Mercury (quicksilver), Saturn (lead), Jupiter (tin), the Moon (silver), Venus (copper), Mars (iron) and the Sun (gold), and the alchemist performs each laboratory procedure according to the rules of its specific planet and metal.

STAGES OF COMPLETION

Alchemical manuscripts differ in their descriptions of laboratory operations. Tasks such as calcination, solution, distillation, separation, fermentation and evaporation are repeated at various stages throughout the work. Often, these procedures are rearranged to confuse unworthy practitioners of the art. Despite repetitions and intentional scrambling, most manuscripts agree that, at some point, the material in the vessel turns black (Nigredo), then white (Albedo), then red (Rubedo). These colours represent significant plateaus and they can be observed by the alchemist through the transparency of the vessel's glass surface. Another stage, called the Peacock's Tail, is an intermediary point when a rainbow, or an iridescence, appears in the vessel. Each of these stages is often illustrated in traditional manuscripts as a bird: the black crow of Nigredo will appear, then the peacock, the white swan of Albedo, and the phoenix of Rubedo, the fiery stage of union and completion.

Mythological gods and goddesses rest within the Earth. The seven planets rule the seven metals through their alchemical transformations as silver, gold, copper, tin, iron, lead and quicksilver.

[19]

Each of these symbols appears in the illustration, below left. The crowned lion symbolizes the fixed masculine aspects of Primal Matter, while the crowned eagle symbolizes its volatile feminine nature. The crowned serpent, like the serpent within the vessel above, is another symbol for Primal Matter, and its potential for perfection. The winged dragon represents both the fire that heats the furnace above and the volatile nature of these operations.

CULMINATION

The culmination of the work, the passionate fusion of the King and Queen, is represented by the Androgyne ~ the refinement of Primal Matter and the union of the masculine and feminine archetypes. First, the White Queen is revived as the Moon, or silver, followed by the Red King, who personifies the Sun and gold. After this 'Chemical Wedding' of the Queen and King, their child, the Philosopher's Stone, is born. This substance is capable of transmuting other metals to silver and gold through a powerful process of multiplication. The Ouroboros, or dragon biting its own tail, represents the cyclic qualities of the work. It serves as a reminder that one already possesses in the beginning what one hopes to achieve, and that, at any stage in the process, a new cycle may soon begin.

LEFT *Beneath the furnace are symbols of the King, Queen, Primal Matter and volatile fire. The crow, peacock, swan and phoenix represent stages of the work.*

ABOVE *The King and Queen are married by a bishop, just as the catalyst Salt joins Philosophic Sulphur and Philosophic Mercury in a Chemical Wedding.*

The Interpretations

THE interpretations that follow cover each of the twenty-eight stones. Below the name of each stone you will find alternative names associated with it, plus key phrases to highlight its meaning in your life. Then follows a description of its role in the laboratory, as well as suggestions about how to adapt its message to your question. Each interpretation also contains an illustration, an engraving taken from an old alchemical text. These images are filled with symbolic objects. They will augment your understanding of alchemy's hidden wisdom and can be studied to aid your interpretation of each message.

Here, as in earlier times, the alchemist's guide is the text. Traditional manuscripts were filled with strange symbols and arcane language, full of puzzles and paradoxes. What exactly is a 'fire that does not burn'? How is the 'Stone of the Philosopher' different from the 'Philosopher's Stone'? These challenges greet every Initiate to the alchemical work, and they force the new practitioner constantly to weigh the message in the text against the intuitive responses of the mind and heart. Likewise, as you begin to work with the alchemy stones, it will be your challenge to interpret the messages received and to find the truest and most applicable meaning of their wisdom in your life. Although it seems that chance plays a major role in selecting these symbols, it is your interpretative skills that are the key to unlocking their wisdom.

Consulting the alchemy stones can be both an amusing pastime or a more serious quest, depending on your needs. As you become more familiar with these symbols, certain ones will take on personal meanings and possibly connections to specific people or situations in your life. Any stone's message may acquire new interpretations over time, and these insights will clearly reflect your own inner process and developing state of mind.

Read through these interpretations carefully and, when you have become familiar with your stones, you will be able to use them in a reading. To do this, read through Part Two and select a reading to suit your situation. For easier identification and reference, there is a visual index of the stones (*see pages 94~5*) so you can immediately find their interpretations.

The dragon bites its tail, signifying unity and cyclic renewal. The Philosopher's

Stone and Primal Matter differ only in their states of perfection.

ALCHEMISTS

1 *Puffer*

Bellows

∘ *Reorganize* ∘ *Reconsider your goals* ∘ *Find the humour in your frustrations*

IN THE LABORATORY

The term 'Puffer' is a comic reference to the alchemist who is full of hot air, like the bellows used to heat the fire in the alchemical furnace, or Athanor. The distinction between Puffers and true alchemical philosophers is based on their motivations. The Puffer, with a rather naïve and misguided understanding of alchemy, wants to 'get rich quick' and uses the alchemical process only as a means to an end. In truth, the attainment of gold is just a by-product of the work. The dedicated alchemical philosopher understands the deeper meaning of alchemy and the quest towards self-perfection that begins when one engages in the work.

FOR YOU

Analyse your motives for reaching your goals and put your desire for material gain into proper perspective. The path to reach what you desire may not be easy. Recognize your weaknesses and learn to laugh at yourself. Correct any mistakes you have made in the past and release the blame you have placed on others.

Begin to observe all aspects of process along your way, rather than concerning yourself only with the end result. Analyse your shortcomings and pay close attention to the real progress you make. Perhaps you need to learn more about your situation, develop your skills or engage in a new programme of study. Seek the deeper, broader and higher aspects of your project and observe how your environment reflects your state of mind. Pay more attention to your inner processes than to the external things about you. Alchemy is an activity that takes place in the physical world, but in your heart this must be a spiritual quest.

*The Puffer, named after the bellows used to control the fiery furnace,
is a foolish alchemist who struggles in chaos, unaware of the clarity of
alchemy's higher path. The disarray in the laboratory reflects this alchemist's
scattered, misguided and confused approach. A re-evaluation of resources
and goals is sorely needed.*

A L C H E M I S T S

2 *Initiate*

New Moon

◦ *Seek new adventures* ◦ *Follow a natural path*
◦ *Let experience be your guide*

IN THE LABORATORY

An Initiate is the alchemist at the beginning of the quest, like the new Moon at the beginning of its cycle. The darkness of a new Moon results when the Moon passes through the shadow of the Earth. Symbolically, this event joins the unconscious lunar mind to the Earth's physical matter. You stand at the beginning of a new alchemical cycle in which your intuition can be used to transform the material world. The Initiate is a seeker, a wanderer along a new path. Follow the footsteps of Nature and look to the natural world for the signs and directions revealed to you.

FOR YOU

New life and light are beginning to grow within. Many secrets have yet to be deciphered and there may be obstacles to overcome. This stage of initiation is a powerful and wondrous time. You might seek a teacher or guide, or gather additional information to help you interpret the signs you encounter along the way. Ultimately, this teacher already exists inside you ~ the more completely you come to know yourself, the more answers you will discover within.

Your intuition and unconscious drives are strongly at work here. Perhaps you are involved in a situation that you do not entirely understand or control. Do not be discouraged if the path ahead seems long and arduous. Keep focused on your goal and your way will be illuminated. Alchemy is always a process of becoming, of searching and new beginnings. Each step contains valuable lessons. Open your eyes, your mind and your heart to what the Universe may offer you along the way, and observe the wisdom in the everyday world around you.

The darkness of the new Moon begins a cycle of discovery. The Initiate is a
new seeker on the path, who follows in the footsteps of Nature.
Nature holds the secrets for growth and renewal ~ she will bring abundant
flowers and fruits in time.

A L C H E M I S T S

3 Adept

Eclipse

° *Trust your skills and abilities* ° *Acknowledge your achievements*

IN THE LABORATORY

The Adept attains wisdom through a careful study of alchemical manuscripts and diligent observation in the laboratory. Success can only be achieved through trial and error. The material result of alchemy is the production of gold and silver, symbolized by a man and a woman, the Sun and the Moon. Its mental equivalent is the perfect union of the conscious and unconscious mind, a fusion of the intuition and the intellect. On a cosmic level, an eclipse represents this conjunction of the Moon and the Sun. The Adept recognizes that these two polarized aspects can be perfected within. And although a full eclipse is rare, its appearance signals the completion of a cycle and a joyful fullness to be celebrated.

FOR YOU

Take pride in your accomplishments. Difficulties and adversities have been overcome in the past. Through your determination, dedication and perseverance, you have reached the goals you set yourself. Draw on these same resources to set new goals for the future. Success is achieved through a careful balance of the intellect and intuition, the industrious and the playful, the worldly and the spiritual. Maintain this balance as you construct future plans. You have acquired much wisdom that can now be shared with others. Ultimately, the knowledge you have gained of yourself will be most helpful in tackling challenges to come. As you celebrate your past achievements, remember that the true alchemical philosopher understands that, on reaching any stage of completion, a new cycle is about to begin. Trust yourself ~ you have the skills you need.

The Adept understands the geometric symbolism of alchemy. The circle represents the unity of matter with its dual male and female aspects; the square shows the stability of the four elements; and the triangle stands for the trinity of body, mind and spirit. To reach the goal, the Adept combines practical skills, intellectual insights and spiritual perfection.

INGREDIENTS AND TOOLS

4 *Primal Matter*

Journey ◦ Descent ◦ Discovery

◦ *The resources you need are all around you ◦ Go deep within to discover what you want*

IN THE LABORATORY

To begin the work, the alchemist's first task is to identify and find Primal Matter. Alchemical manuscripts suggest that this enigmatic substance is everywhere, like the Earth and the Air that surround us; yet its identity alludes all but the most perceptive seekers. Often the alchemical quest begins with a journey, as the Initiate sets out to find this substance. Because Primal Matter is equated with the Earth, some seek it underground, in caves or mines. Others say that it exists in the everyday world and must simply be recognized.

Primal Matter exists in a raw and unrefined state, but it contains all that is necessary to achieve perfection. The search for this substance must occur both in the world and within oneself.

FOR YOU

You must identify what you are seeking and analyse clearly the problems to be solved before you can begin striving for an outcome. As the Initiate descends underground into a mine or cavern to search for Primal Matter, descend into yourself and recognize that you already possess what you are seeking. Do not be driven by superficial desires, but discover what your deeper motivations may be. Trust your own inner strengths to solve any problem, for the key is within. The solution need not be complicated ~ strive for simplicity. Accept the most obvious answer to your question and use the resources at hand to begin the task of self-transformation. Recognition of your own potential is more useful than an endless search for some magical solution. Use your powers of observation to see clearly the task at hand.

[28]

Some say Primal Matter is found deep in the Earth. Others say that it is
everywhere, but only the observant eye can find it. Cubes symbolize the
stability of the four elements.

INGREDIENTS AND TOOLS

5 *Philosophic Sulphur*

Sun King ◦ *Red Rose*

◦ *Energetic action, properly directed, brings new strength, power and courage* ◦ *Think logically, illuminated by the Sun's golden light*

IN THE LABORATORY

The Sun is the King, and symbolizes Philosophic Sulphur, the masculine principle. It represents the active states of matter, filled with energy, embodying its warm, dry and fixed properties. Philosophic Sulphur is combined with Philosophic Mercury in its raw state as Primal Matter. Alchemical operations separate and purify these two properties, refining and balancing the dryness and fixity of Philosophic Sulphur. Eventually the red rose appears, heralding the arrival of the King and the production of gold.

FOR YOU

Philosophic Sulphur represents a masculine quality shared by all people, male and female. It is the active, energetic principle which must be balanced. Do not be too rigid in your stance, but be aware that a strength of purpose will enable you to achieve what you desire.

As impurities are removed from Primal Matter, know that at the beginning of any project you must discard behaviour that has proved unsuccessful in the past. Temper any impetuous, brash and reckless activities and limit your attempts to manipulate the outcome. Let go of any preconceived notions as you become more willing to engage in the process of change. Approach your questions logically with intensity and power. Engage fully in all aspects of the question and stand firm in your resolve. Negotiate from a position of strength, knowing that you have a great reserve of energy. Take a courageous stand. Your authority will be drawn from the deep, red warmth of your heart, as you let your own gold emerge.

[30]

The red rose signals the final perfection of Philosophic Sulphur, as the Sun King reappears wearing brilliant red robes and a golden crown.

INGREDIENTS AND TOOLS

6 Philosophic Mercury

Moon Queen ◦ White Rose

◦ *Receive the creativity and intuitions of your unconscious mind*
◦ *Beauty and grace blossom in the Moon's silvery reflections*

IN THE LABORATORY

Philosophic Mercury is the feminine principle, symbolized by a woman or the Moon. She represents the receptive states of matter, embodying its cool, moist and volatile properties. In its unrefined state within Primal Matter, Philosophic Mercury is combined with its masculine counterpart, Philosophic Sulphur. After repeated alchemical operations, they are separated and Philosophic Mercury is refined into silver. When the Queen reappears, an event symbolized by the white rose, she is crowned with silver and wears white robes, sometimes covered with antique lace and rare pearls.

FOR YOU

Philosophic Mercury is a feminine quality shared universally ~ we can all develop our receptive abilities. This principle provides increasing insight and intuition when its fluid volatility is activated and balanced. Your best approach may begin with deep, inner reflection. You will be nurtured by the immense power of your uncon‑ scious feelings. Emotional reactions hold great value and may prove more useful than objective assessments of the situation. Even so, do not let yourself be over‑ whelmed by your emotions or by volatile overreaction to a situation. Every problem has a solution in time, and your own quiet persistence may be the most effective way of achieving change. Creative intuition is the key. As the white rose unfolds its beauty in the moonlight, draw your inspiration from peaceful and profound inner contemplation. Let your inner light shine on those around you, just as the silver Moon pierces the darkness of the night.

[32]

Medicina alba sive Eli-
xir album.

The Moon is the Queen, perfected from the raw material of Philosophic
Mercury. The white rose signals her appearance and the production of silver.

INGREDIENTS AND TOOLS

7 *Salt*

Mercury's Caduceus ◦ Catalyst

◦ *Observe the situation from a distance ◦ Serve as a facilitator for solving problems ◦ Bring opposing forces together*

IN THE LABORATORY

Paracelsus, a pioneering Renaissance alchemist and physician, revealed that Salt is the mysterious third substance needed as a catalyst to join together the two opposing properties of Philosophic Sulphur and Philosophic Mercury. This catalyst is represented by the god Mercury holding his caduceus, with its two coiled snakes wrapped around a central staff to represent the harmonious conjunction of opposites. It is only in the presence of this catalyst that the Sun King and Moon Queen are combined as one.

FOR YOU

Oppositions impede resolution. Confusion exists over which path to take, for each leads you toward a different course of action. You are pulled in two directions and need guidance in deciding where to focus your energies. The role of the catalyst Salt can provide insight. Facilitating, networking and making connections between forces may be a better approach than your active participation in battle. Your quiet presence in this process will begin to make a difference. You, or perhaps another person, might serve as a facilitator to resolve any problems. You may also find yourself acting as a cohesive force keeping the scattered parts of a project or group of people together. Weigh the alternatives, identify the best aspects of each option, then bring opposing forces together in a new synthesis. Your detached oversight may be all that is needed to finalize a project. As a physician, Paracelsus also strove to find practical, medicinal uses for alchemical products, so remember that the resolution of external oppositions can nurture your inner self and begin the healing process.

[34]

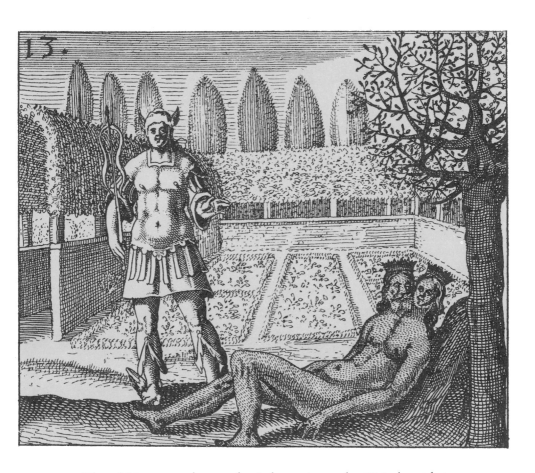

*The god Mercury watches over the Androgyne in a garden. He is the catalyst
Salt who brings the King and Queen together like the two serpents who
twine around his caduceus staff.*

INGREDIENTS AND TOOLS

8 Alembic

Vessel ∘ Philosophic Egg

∘ *Observe what you have set in motion* ∘ *Patiently wait for the outcome* ∘ *Careful evaluation will help you recognize when to act*

IN THE LABORATORY

Alchemical operations take place in the Alembic, a transparent glass vessel. After the initial operations are complete, both observation of the occurrences within the vessel and careful timing are crucial. Success will come only if the proper ingredients are found and the correct procedures are followed. The alchemist watches for certain colours to appear in the turbulent battles and purifying inundations of the process ~ black, an iridescent rainbow, white and, finally, red. These colours signal the completion of important stages by which the success of the work can be gauged.

FOR YOU

Through watchful supervision, success can be achieved. Events have been set in motion; now patient observation may be the best approach. You have applied your wisdom and experience, so must now let the process take its natural course of evolution. Timing is important: know when to observe and when to intervene. Shaking the vessel or stirring its contents does little to help the process for the alchemist at this point. Similarly, constant worrying and obsessing about a problem cannot change it. If the expected results do not appear, the process must be revised and repeated. Perhaps there is a missing ingredient or there has been a misunderstanding of what is required. Do not despair. Wisdom is gained from unsuccessful experiments.

The glass of the Alembic is both a transparent and a reflective surface. While observing the contents in the interior, the alchemist is reflected on to the glass surface of the vessel. Likewise, be aware that what you observe in your environment mirrors your own inner process.

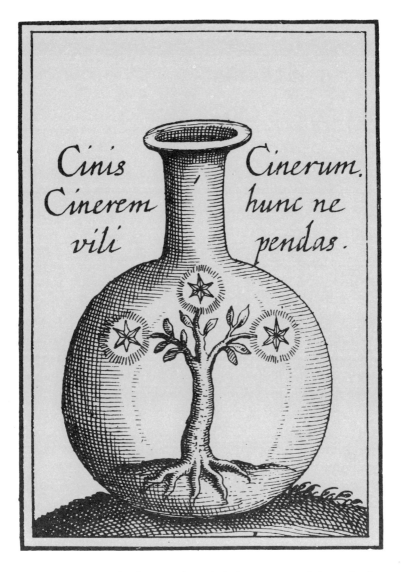

Cinis Cinerum.
Cinerem hunc ne
vili pendas.

The Alembic is the glass vessel in which the operations of the work take place. Because of its rounded interior, it is also known as the 'Philosophic Egg'. Through its transparent surface the alchemist observes the work progressing like a young tree rooting and sprouting in the Earth.

INGREDIENTS   AND   TOOLS

9 *Athanor*

Furnace

∘ *Feel the strength and protection of the forces surrounding you*
∘ *Begin applying heat to your project* ∘ *Act with care and moderation*

IN THE LABORATORY

The Athanor is the furnace that holds and heats the alchemical vessel. It is usually built of solid brick with vents to control the fire inside. Heat is one of the most important elements of the work. Gentle heating and cooling causes gases and liquids to rise and fall in the vessel during distillation and condensation. Like a hen incubating her eggs, the alchemist must keep the heat inside the vessel, or 'Philosophic Egg', at a stable temperature. It is this heating process that eventually brings about the conjunction of Philosophic Sulphur and Philosophic Mercury ~ the King and Queen, joined in their 'Chemical Wedding'.

FOR YOU

In order to cook something properly or to initiate a new course of action, a fire must be lit, watched, fanned and kept alight. Action must be taken now if you want to ignite new energies. Activity is called for, but it must be applied with moderation. You are in control of the situation, so there is no need to overheat or to overreact. Know that, like the brick Athanor furnace, you are supported by a solid base and insulated walls, with a gentle warming fire within. Perhaps there are opposing viewpoints that need reconciliation. If so, energetic action, moderated by warm compassion, can lead to resolution; or venting can be helpful to cool a fiery temper. Remember that, along with heating, cooling the furnace is essential to 'cook' the substances in the vessel properly. Like the alchemist, observe when the 'egg' of your project begins to cool, then turn it gently to be warmed by the heat radiating from your heart.

The god Mercury and the lion of Primal Matter stand beside the Athanor furnace which holds three vessels. The vents aid in proper heating and cooling.

E L E M E N T S

10 *Earth*

Lion

○ *Identify exactly what you need* ○ *Be practical in your approach*
○ *Stand firm and build the foundations to realize your plans*

IN THE LABORATORY

In its diversity, Earth appears as grains of sand on a beach, warm loamy garden soil, tough clay on a mountainside or huge solid boulders. It is the element most closely equated with Primal Matter, although all substances to some degree contain Earth's qualities of dryness and solidity. The lion, its symbol, represents its fixed aspects, while two lions, male and female, can represent the two opposing properties of Primal Matter. Alchemical processes duplicate the Earth's natural cycle in its evolution of death and rebirth. Seeds must be buried in the Earth before new life can begin and, as they germinate and take root, the Earth's minerals support the life of the plant to maturity. The Earth then receives back the mature plant so that it can decay and replenish its fertility.

FOR YOU

Whatever the physical appearance of the Earth, it is a solid substance that can be depended on for support. Feel yourself grounded in the world, let your feet touch the cool grass, knowing that layers of soil and bedrock are beneath you. Approach decisions with this grounding in the real world. Look for practical solutions and straightforward, down-to-earth approaches. Although material gain should not be your only consideration, this may be the time to think about the realistic financial aspects of your position. Weigh the situation carefully, as if you were holding a real object in your hand. In the midst of conflict, stand firm in your resolve. Although we sometimes take the Earth for granted, the enormity of this solid supportive sub-stance should be acknowledged and used to support your own inner strength.

The lion represents the element Earth, ruling over practical matters and material possessions. His four paws rest on the ground to indicate its stability.

E L E M E N T S

11 *Water*

Mermaid

∘ *Events can flow effortlessly* ∘ *Adapt, be patient and remain persistent* ∘ *Feel your emotions and release them*

IN THE LABORATORY

The element Water represents those aspects of matter that are moist, fluid and humid. It is connected closely to the phase of ablution, when Primal Matter is washed of all impurities. During the operations of distillation, Water evaporates and falls as condensation in the Alembic vessel, further refining the substance. This element is traditionally connected to love and the emotions.

FOR YOU

As our watery planet floats in space, huge cloud-crowned oceans swell and fall under the influence of the Moon. From the joyous bubbling of a mountain stream and the cascading veil of a waterfall, to the deep surging power of rivers and the eternal give and take of ocean waves, Water holds many lessons. Its turbulent tempests and dangerous undertows show it to be a powerful force. It dances around, over, under and through any obstacles encountered as it continues its path to the sea. In its persistence and timeless endurance, it can carve canyons, and through its gentle action can smooth the hardest surfaces into fluid forms.

The fluidity of Water in all its various forms can be emulated with great success. Adaptability and conformity within boundaries may be the proper approach for now, knowing that your unending persistence will eventually wear away any resistance. Water is patient and powerful at the same time. Like a sudden rain shower, a release of emotions can be helpful to relieve stress and clear out old debris. In quiet reflection, sink into that deep well of feeling within and intuitively draw up a course for proper action.

[42]

The element of Water is represented by a nurturing woman and a fish.
She rules over the emotions and the spheres of love and happiness.

E L E M E N T S

12 *Air*

Eagle

∘ *Mental clarity brings transformation* ∘ *Soar high and explore a limitless Universe* ∘ *Enjoy your freedom*

IN THE LABORATORY

Air is the life-giving force joining the Earth and the heavens. As one aspect of Primal Matter, it represents those qualities that are subtle and gaseous. The gases in the vessel are symbolized by rising and falling birds; as liquids boil, gases escape and coalesce like crystallized birds on the walls of the vessel. Air is connected to the intellect and to the life of the mind, which must moderate physical activity just as the careful addition of Air is used to moderate fire and its effects in the laboratory.

FOR YOU

A gentle breeze stirs the newly formed leaves in spring to encourage their unfolding and growth. Immense swirling currents of Air encircle the planet and direct the weather, bringing both rain and clearing sunshine. Although Air is a subtle force, it can cause great transformation and metamorphosis.

Change is possible through a careful exercising of your mental powers, even though your presence may seem invisible. Before any action is taken, allow time for reflection. Spontaneous ideas and deliberate plans both have a function in this process. As gases escape from boiling liquid, you may need to remove yourself if the activity around gets too hectic. You have the freedom and mobility to act, but too many possibilities may be clouding your line of vision. Clear, sharp perceptions gained at some distance from the situation are needed here. Just as gases are released to purify the substance in the process of distillation, removal of all unessential factors is necessary to find the essence of your solution. Exhale all negative thoughts and breathe in the peacefulness, love and joy that surround us all.

Two eagles fly into the Air from their nest atop a mountain.
They are close to the sky and represent the realm of the mind and its
powers of transformation. Take flight and begin to explore the limitless
possibilities around you.

E L E M E N T S

13 *Fire*

Salamander

◦ *Thrive in the midst of adversity* ◦ *Vigorous action brings transformation*

IN THE LABORATORY

Fire is the agent of transformation. Full of energy and activity, it represents those aspects of matter that are hot and dry. Heating with Fire occurs both inside and outside the vessel: internal Fire is created when acids react together to elevate the temperature within the vessel and break down the materials; an external Fire, contained within the Athanor furnace, heats the vessel and causes Philosophic Sulphur and Philosophic Mercury to unite. Although care must be taken to control its power, Fire is an essential tool. The alchemist must create a constant gentle heat and a uniform temperature within the vessel for the great work to succeed. The substance in the vessel can withstand the heating process, like the mythic salamander who can survive Fire unharmed.

FOR YOU

The Fire within your heart is capable of transforming the world both inside and out. Use your initiative, inventiveness and spontaneity to set new projects in motion. Now is the time for action applied carefully and consistently to those areas in your life where it is needed. Like the salamander, you can survive external adversity and actually thrive, even when the situation around you is overheated and inflamed. Your energy now burns brightly, but take some care to keep new fires under control.

Fire can both break down matter and fuse it; so, too, can your passion create the necessary changes for letting go of destructive elements in your life and bringing union with new, beneficial ones. Warmth and compassion given to others will return to you threefold when you need it most.

*The salamander can live within Fire. This element represents the
unlimited transformational energy available to all.*

E L E M E N T S

14 Quintessence

Six-pointed Star

◦ *Balance your energies and feel the peace of equilibrium* ◦ *Cosmic forces bring effortless change when you release limiting thoughts*

IN THE LABORATORY

The Quintessence is that enigmatic suspension that holds all the other elements ~ Earth, Water, Air and Fire ~ together in a perfect balance. Its symbol, a six-pointed star, is formed by superimposing the triangular symbols of the other four elements over one another to represent their unification. The Quintessence is the combination of gold and light, perfected matter and energy, representing the balance and equilibrium that will unite the King and Queen.

FOR YOU

The Quintessence calls for a cosmic unification, a joining of all your forces towards a single goal. Use the best qualities contained in each element to your best advantage ~ the solid groundedness of the Earth, the fluid adaptability of Water, the volatile transformational aspects of the Air and the energetic fusing capacity of Fire. Practical preparation, emotional engagement, intellectual planning and physical action are all necessary to complete your goal. Combine and consolidate your resources. Consider all possible paths before deciding your proper course of action. As precious stones and crystals are formed through the interactions of Earth, Water, Air and Fire, the process of their fusion can be either cataclysmic or of long, slow duration. Decide if short-range or long-range goals are the most vital now.

You have many choices. As you weigh the various components, consider how best a balance can be achieved. This may be the opportunity to combine all the talents you have nurtured in the past and to transform them into a perfect equilibrium of body, mind and soul.

[48]

The Quintessence is an ethereal substance holding the four elements in perfect suspension. Here a beautiful young woman is borne on the Water like the goddess Venus rising from the sea foam. With her crown of six-pointed stars, she appears weightless and serene between the Sun and the Moon.

P L A N E T S   A N D   M E T A L S

15 *Mercury*

Quicksilver

∘ *Volatile new ideas can yield great results* ∘ *Be prepared to go through rapid and dramatic changes* ∘ *Communicate with those who can help*

IN THE LABORATORY

Mercury is the closest planet to the sun and it oversees the realms of the intellect and communication. Like the metal quicksilver, it is represented by the god of travel, Mercury, messenger of the gods, whose sacred sites were marked by stones along the road. Thus, the god rules the Initiate's journey to find Primal Matter and to decode the many curious symbols and phrases found in alchemical manuscripts. The planet then exerts its influence over the initial operations of the work. This is a gaseous stage when the matter starts to darken and sinks to the bottom of the vessel in preparation for the dramatic stages to come.

FOR YOU

Your challenge is knowing what to look for and where to begin. As the planet Mercury rules the intellect and learning ability, it will be of great aid as you increase your capacity to identify problems. You are facing an exciting time when many choices and paths will open up to you. Your curiosity is highlighted as you begin to walk in a new direction. Learn to recognize and decipher all the signs along the way, and communicate with those who can best aid your progress. You can foresee and avoid potential problems with the aid of a sharp mind. Your solutions will be spontaneous and innovative, so trust any brilliant flashes of inspiration that you might have. However, if too many different possibilities present themselves, take care to order your priorities. New, exciting plans may appear feasible, but then evaporate quickly. Balance can be achieved if you harmonize your material needs with your spiritual path, and ground both in the world of reality.

Mercury has multiple meanings: the feminine principle is Philosophic Mercury, while Salt is represented by the god Mercury. The alchemist understands this, and that it must be present in two forms at the start. It then governs the first stage of the work as the substance in the vessel undergoes rapid changes and vapours rise, condense and fall back in volatile succession.

P L A N E T S   A N D   M E T A L S

16 Saturn

Lead

◦ *Discard destructive habits* ◦ *Recover from the chaos of the past*
◦ *Time heals all wounds*

IN THE LABORATORY

In the ancient world, Saturn was thought to be the most distant planet from the Earth. Its slow movements in deep space suggested a dull, plodding, heavy planet associated with cold and darkness. In mythology, the god Saturn, who represents the planet, was tricked into swallowing a rock which he eventually expelled. Likewise, lead, the metal governed by Saturn, must be cleansed of impurities. The most base of all metals, lead is dense, chaotic and furthest away from the purity of gold. The planet oversees the operations at the beginning of the alchemical work, when lead is symbolically destroyed: it melts, boils and finally solidifies. When the stage of Nigredo is reached, the substance is blacker than the blackest night.

FOR YOU

At the beginning of the process of self-change, it is necessary to recognize those aspects of your life that must be destroyed or expelled in order for real growth to begin. Often this purging creates a great upheaval, bringing up fears of isolation and loneliness. These are deeply felt anxieties, perhaps deriving from family issues. The dull, heavy aspects of the planet Saturn mirror habits and addictions that keep you locked into old patterns. This is a time of introspection, of sinking into yourself to identify the things that need changing by facing your deepest fears. The first step towards profound change is to recognize harmful aspects of your behaviour. Hard work may be involved, facing difficulties and learning from adversity. Movement may be slow, but deep transformational processes are at work. The coloured rings of Saturn reveal the cosmic protection surrounding you as you begin to heal yourself.

*The god Saturn holds a scythe, both a weapon and a tool for harvesting.
Because of his own fear of death, Saturn devoured all of his children. His
son Jupiter was saved through his mother's clever trick of substituting a rock
for the infant. The rock was expelled when Saturn was purged and the other
children were freed as well.*

P L A N E T S   A N D   M E T A L S

17 *Jupiter*

Tin

○ *Dawn breaks, bringing hope and new beginnings* ○ *Wisdom is rising* ○ *Expand your powers and receive abundance*

IN THE LABORATORY

Jupiter is the largest of the planets, revered for its weight and massiveness, and for its power to bring opportunity and growth on the earthly plane. It is associated with tin, a malleable and ductile material that combines with copper as an alloy to produce bronze. As the mythological son of Saturn, Jupiter's planetary influence in alchemical operations occurs just after Saturn's reign. Thus, Jupiter is associated with the dawn that follows the night. Water begins this process of purification ~ vapours and rains are abundant in the vessel and condensation appears on the surface. Blackened Primal Matter begins to turn lighter shades of grey, as Jupiter stands midway between lead and silver, between Saturn and the Moon.

FOR YOU

Light begins to return after a period of darkness. Personal isolation is diminished now as you move into a wider sphere of activity where many new opportunities for growth will be revealed. During this period of transformation, your adaptability and capacity for change will be a great asset. Consider the strengths that Jupiter offers as an alloy with Venus (copper) ~ discovering the loving and intuitive side of your nature can strengthen the qualities you already possess. As new abundance manifests, remember to practise moderation. Alchemy is a spiritual quest that can be derailed by an overemphasis on material acquisitions. Healing benefits will be showered on you, so remember to share your good fortune with humility and generosity. A cosmic expansion supports and augments your self-transformation. As new ideas and insights spring to mind, lovingly observe your process of growth.

[54]

*Jupiter is accompanied by an eagle, a symbol of feminine volatility, and he has
many legendary associations with the feminine, as he loved women and often
transformed himself in order to achieve union with them. His daughter
Minerva, known as Athena in ancient Greece, is the goddess of wisdom who
springs fully grown from his head. The masculine and feminine must be
separated before each can reach their full potential.*

[55]

PLANETS AND METALS

18 Moon

Diana ∘ Silver

∘ *Your intuition can tap unconscious resources* ∘ *Listen to your dreams* ∘ *Imagine the possibilities* ∘ *Remain receptive to change*

IN THE LABORATORY

In the ancient world, the Moon was believed to be a planet. Within its monthly cycle, it transforms rapidly through its new, waxing, full and waning stages. Because of its close proximity to the Earth, the Moon exerts a powerful influence, controlling the tides, planting, and even pregnancy and harvest. Connected to the night and to the world of dreams, it also symbolizes the powerful forces of the unconscious mind.

Moon goddesses like Diana represent purity and self-sufficiency and, after the reign of Jupiter, the Moon oversees additional washings that purify the substance in the vessel until it achieves a brilliant whiteness. The feminine property of Philosophic Mercury is perfected and silver is created. The Moon is the mother of the Philosopher's Stone and provides her child with gentle care and nurturing love.

FOR YOU

The depths of your instincts will guide you through rapid change and cyclic renewal. The fertile generation of ideas, fulfilment of dreams and letting go of disappointments revolve with ever-increasing speed in your life. Maintain your receptivity to the flow of the Universe.

The Moon strongly exerts its power over the body, so be in touch with all your physical aspects. Periods of energetic activity should be followed by adequate rest and relaxation. As the Moon's rhythms influence your life, feel, listen and respond. Your imagination is activated now and will provide you with many gifts of inspiration. Trust your deepest intuitive impulses. Celebrate reaching a plateau in which body and soul flow as one and are attuned to the cycles of nature.

The Moon is silver and the mother of the Philosopher's Stone. Earth,
Water, Fire and Air are all symbolized here nurturing the process of birth.
Many cultures associate the Moon with fertility, representing the lifespan
from innocence, through maturity, to old age.

P L A N E T S A N D M E T A L S

19 *Venus*

Copper

○ *Surround yourself with beauty* ○ *Explore your creativity* ○ *Indulge your passions* ○ *Share your love and receive love in return*

IN THE LABORATORY

The planet Venus is close to the Earth and the Moon, and appears as the morning or evening star, heralding the transitions between night and day, darkness and light. It is associated with copper, a malleable metal with excellent conductivity. Following the influence of the Moon and the attainment of silver, the matter in the vessel passes from white, through green, to a pale plum-blue and then on to a reddish-brown associated with copper. The colour of gold is suggested, but not yet attained. During this phase, the matter in the vessel sinks and swells in rapid continuous cycles within a moist environment. While the alchemical Venus can be volatile, her influence is tender and gentle as she stirs the emotions and brings new love.

FOR YOU

Surround yourself with the people and things you love, creating an environment of peace, harmony and serenity. Fill your home with simple things of great beauty, like fresh flowers and works of art. Conditions are favourable to pursue those things that you desire most. The goal of alchemy extends far beyond the narrow pursuit of wealth, for our truest riches are cherished loves and friendships. Nurture your creativity and indulge your instincts towards communication and union. Emotional upheavals in the past may have caused feelings of instability. A new openness to love, both of the self and of others, begins the process of healing. The conductivity of copper suggests the unimpeded flow of Venus's compassion, just as unconditional love is given and received effortlessly. Reinforce connections with positive forces in your life and passionately engage in activities that best nourish your growth.

Venus, the goddess of love, supports the quest for beauty, harmony and
sensuality. She governs the volatile processes that quicken the amorous
passion necessary to reunite the masculine and feminine. Here she embraces
Mercury while the Androgyne rises above them.

PLANETS AND METALS

20 *Mars*

Iron

◦ *Control anger and unruly emotions* ◦ *Direct your energy towards positive action* ◦ *Bravely take risks* ◦ *Act courageously and vigorously*

IN THE LABORATORY

The planet Mars is an active force in our lives, strengthening our energy, creativity and sex drive. Associated in ancient times with agricultural rituals and war, it supports our dynamic growth as well as our battles with adversity. Your inner strength can emerge as a powerful tool capable of fusing the spiritual and physical aspects in your life. Mars is associated with iron, a heavy, magnetic metal that rusts in moist air. It is found in igneous rocks, those forged through fire. In the alchemical process, Mars's influence follows the reign of Venus. Matter in the vessel dries and changes from orange to yellow-brown, finally transforming into the colours of the rainbow. Fire, applied with moderation and precision, eliminates the cooler, fluid aspects of the matter and solidifies its masculine components, intensifying the colour red.

FOR YOU

Using the sword of your courage and will, attack your problems head-on. Identify your deepest needs and assert them now. Indecision caused by conflicting emotions can be cleared by an objective assessment of the situation and by acting aggressively to initiate positive change. Difficulties in life may have hardened you, like iron which is forged in fire. Moderate any anger that you might feel towards those who have wronged you in the past. Your inner capacity for survival will far outweigh any damage caused by others. Mars will support the healing process needed to overcome afflictions. Armed with what you have learned and conquered in the past, now is the time to act. Your dreams and ambitions can be realized if you seek new challenges and pursue them with determination.

Mars is the god of war, whose sword indicates direct action as he stands poised above the vessel, or Philosophic Egg. The strike of his sword symbolizes the purifying fire that heats the vessel.

P L A N E T S   A N D   M E T A L S

21 Sun

Apollo ∘ Gold

∘ *Let your radiant energy and strength inspire others* ∘ *Light and lead the way* ∘ *Happiness and fulfilment can be attained*

IN THE LABORATORY

In alchemy, the Sun oversees the culmination of the work, signalling the attainment of gold and the rebirth of the King. Perfected from Philosophic Sulphur, he arises radiantly from his tomb ready to take command and lead the way. The symbol for gold shown on the stone represents the connection between the macrocosm and the microcosm, for the circle and the point are one. In the ancient world, the Sun was thought to be a planet revolving around the Earth. The Egyptian goddess Nut gives birth to the Sun every morning, while the Greek god Apollo brings it to the Earth each day in his chariot. The Sun's daily cycle across the sky lights the way as you proceed on your chosen path. It is the giver of life, warming the planet, its winds and its oceans. As the red globe rises higher in the sky, it transforms into a brilliant gold. Likewise, each day it is possible to create gold in your life.

FOR YOU

The Sun supports the quest for self-knowledge, which is the ultimate goal of alchemy. Self-awareness can bring confidence and purposeful direction to life. After difficult trials and emotional challenges, your courage and strength now shine through. A new joyous vitality and happiness fill your spirit as you get in touch with the healing, higher Self within. The Sun also rules the heart, wherein lies all the warmth needed to bring joy and fulfilment. In the early morning, it evaporates the dew on the rose and opens the mature blossom with its warmth. In this fullness of your development, feel now the warmth of your heart, acknowledge your achievements and allow all the layers of your being to unfold in the light of day.

Apollo is a fiery god who brings the Sun each morning, and represents the gold which is purified from the lion of Primal Matter.

S T A G E S   O F   C O M P L E T I O N

22 Nigredo

Putrefaction ∘ Black Crow

∘ *Night descends* ∘ *Reduce down to essentials and concentrate your efforts* ∘ *Hibernate to recuperate and to recover your inner strength*

IN THE LABORATORY

In the initial operations of the alchemical work, Primal Matter must be destroyed. First it is pulverized, mixed with the secret fire and newly gathered dew. Then it is placed in the vessel where, after a long process of decay, the two opposing properties, Philosophic Sulphur and Philosophic Mercury, are both dissolved and the matter putrefies. When the stage of Nigredo is achieved, the substance is darker than the darkest night. The black crow or raven marks this point, when the process of rebirth can begin.

FOR YOU

Life's challenges can feel like blows that pulverize the spirit. The death encountered here is not a physical death, but rather it might be experienced as a separation, abandonment of outworn behaviour or letting go of old destructive patterns. Plants die after producing their seeds, which are buried in the ground, storing precious energy. During the darkest days of winter, these seeds begin to germinate, thus completing Nature's cycle. So, too, this dark night of the soul will produce new growth in time. At no other moment are you more deeply in touch with your will to survive. The darkness of night can be terrifying, but it can also bring blessed sleep and relief from the day's troubles. Perhaps the most peaceful time of life is experienced in the darkness of the womb as life's potential begins to take form. The winter solstice, the darkest day of the year, brings hope and the return of the Sun's life. Likewise, your darkest moments hold the power of healing. Conserve your energies. Sink deep into your inner Self to find that seed of new life.

The stage of Nigredo is symbolized by a crow or raven: black birds of prey that feed on carrion and aid in the process of destruction and transformation. It strips the matter down to the bones in this operation of putrefaction ~ Primal Matter is destroyed and the vessel turns black as night.

STAGES   OF   COMPLETION

23 Peacock's Tail

Rainbow

∘ *Opportunities appear abundant* ∘ *Nourish your hopes and dreams, but stay focused and beware of illusions*

IN THE LABORATORY

Like a star appearing in the dark of the night, the volatile principle, a metallic, humid substance, begins to appear in the darkness of Nigredo. Swirling from above, alchemical winds are activated and, within the vessel, the purifying celestial Air falls on the Earth below. As the outer fire is slowly intensified, moisture begins to evaporate until the matter is coagulated below. A Peacock's Tail of beautiful iridescent colours appears like a rainbow after a storm.

FOR YOU

The time has come after a period of darkness to emerge again into the light of day. You may feel that you are waking from a deep sleep or from a necessary period of rest and recuperation. Cosmic winds begin to stir your spirits, signalling a call for personal change. Spring has arrived and new shoots are bursting forth with the potential for abundant growth. Careful pruning now will ensure a healthy harvest later. New possibilities appear on the horizon like the myriad of colours in the rainbow. Take care not to rush headlong into illusion. The rainbow promises a pot of gold, but seems to fade when we chase after it.

External forces may have encouraged this change, but you know best your own timetable for transformation. Honour your inner cycles and emerge gently from the cocoon. Remember that the new wings of a butterfly need time to dry in the sun before taking flight. Acknowledge past achievements with pride, while humbly realizing there is still more to accomplish and learn. As the peacock displays its beautiful tail, begin to open and share your wondrous inner perfection with the world.

*A rainbow appears after a storm. Clouds break open and sunlight returns.
So, too, the Peacock's Tail is an intermediate stage when the glistening
colours of the rainbow appear iridescent in the vessel.*

[67]

S T A G E S   O F   C O M P L E T I O N

24 *Albedo*

Purification ○ White Swan

○ *Wash away all debris* ○ *Eliminate distractions and dissolve fixed attitudes* ○ *Tap the deep well of your emotions and intuition*

IN THE LABORATORY

Albedo is the phase of washing and purification. The matter in the vessel gradually whitens in a series of inundations that dissolve its fixed aspects and remove impurities. Whiteness first appears as a thin circle that enlarges until the whole substance turns a brilliant white, indicating its strength to withstand the ardour of the fire to come. The elegant white swan has emerged to glide gracefully across the water. In Western cultures, the colour white is a symbol of innocence, often worn by brides at weddings. Indeed, a marriage or reunion is at hand. In previous operations, Philosophic Sulphur and Philosophic Mercury have been separated, destroyed and laid to rest. They are now dissolved in the cleansing waters that bring them back to life. The Moon Queen appears first and prepares to be reunited with her beloved.

FOR YOU

Letting go of fixed attitudes is the secret in this process of dissolution. Albedo achieves a level of perfect fluidity, teaching us how to flow effortlessly with life. Like a grain of sand within the oyster, adversity has offered you an opportunity for transformation. Deep within your core, there is a brilliant white jewel, a pearl of immense worth, waiting to emerge. Its layers have been formed through the washings of repeated waves of emotion, fortified by your own ability to heal yourself and transform hardships into personal strength. Dissolved in the healing waters of Albedo, the alchemical Queen regains her spirit. Likewise, by sinking into a meditative peace, you allow your intuitive feelings to rise. As the flood of inspiration recedes, the path to follow will emerge clear and glistening before you.

Albedo is the stage when all impurities are washed away. The cleansing water is described as a tempest, a flood or a fiery laundry that swells over the matter and gradually recedes, revealing a new form. Light has returned after darkness, life has returned after death.

STAGES OF COMPLETION

25 *Rubedo*

Conjunction ∘ Red Phoenix

∘ *Love and pleasure surround you* ∘ *Reunions are imminent*
∘ *Passionately join with others* ∘ *Conceive new plans*

IN THE LABORATORY

The red phase of Rubedo begins with the Chemical Wedding in which the Sun King and the Moon Queen are united. On their wedding night, the vessel is heated to increase their passion and the two join together in the fires of love. After trials and tribulations, their ordeals are over and love fills the vessel. As fixed Philosophic Sulphur and volatile Philosophic Mercury unite, the matter dries completely and is transformed into a brilliant-red powder. This reunion fills them with joy as their intense passion for each other draws them close. Within this red heat, they conceive their child, the Philosopher's Stone. The red phoenix rises from the flames like the child born in the fiery furnace.

FOR YOU

As the phoenix survives the fire and rises from the ashes, you are emerging triumphant from troubles experienced in the past. The King symbolizes your strength and passionate intensity for life and love. The Queen represents your receptivity to change and the inner powers you possess to create new opportunities and to give them form. This stage in the work indicates balance within the body. Now is the time to resume physical activities that you have enjoyed in the past, and to indulge yourself in pleasurable pursuits. Acknowledge a new sense of wholeness within yourself and nurture its growth with supportive relationships. Reunions are likely: a friend, lover or family member will appear to offer support and companionship. You can experience an equilibrium of mind and body, balancing work and play. This is the beginning of an incredibly fertile time, pregnant with potential for beginning new projects that will bear abundant fruit in the future.

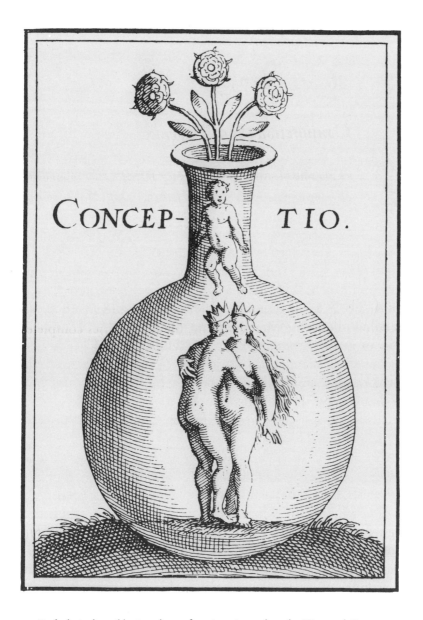

*Rubedo is the reddening phase of conjunction, when the King and Queen
make love and conceive their child, the Philosopher's Stone.*

C U L M I N A T I O N

26 Androgyne

Oneness ◦ Fusion

◦ *Oppositions dissolve* ◦ *Bring the intellect and intuition into perfect alignment* ◦ *Success comes by focusing your energies on a single goal*

IN THE LABORATORY

This summation of the work is represented by the Androgyne, a single figure, combining the Sun and Moon. Both silver and gold are perfected here, each balanced with its opposite. The Androgyne's message is its singular unity, indicating that this phase is most deeply about the Self reaching its full potential.

The symbol of this stone combines the Sun with all phases of the Moon, creating a visual eclipse. Just as the world was created from initial chaos, beginning by separating the darkness from the light, so too the Sun and Moon have been refined from Primal Matter. By duplicating the process of the world's creation, the alchemist begins to glimpse the divine perfection, touching the higher Self and experiencing unconditional love.

FOR YOU

Surviving upheavals, disappointments, isolation and loneliness, you have reached a high plateau of resolution and self-knowledge. Recognize how these trials of the past have taught important lessons and made you the person you are today. Conflicts and oppositions are resolved. Your struggles in the past have helped to forge a new oneness within, causing a rebirth through which you can experience your true higher Self. Intellect and intuition, conscious thoughts and unconscious dreams are joined. Keeping focused on your goals will help direct your path to success. The clarity of the Sun and the visions of the Moon combine to lead you directly to your goals through a balance of the conscious and unconscious mind. Experience the wholeness of your being and open the gate to your expanding spiritual growth.

The Androgyne joins equally as the Sun and Moon, the King and Queen, Philosophic Sulphur and Philosophic Mercury. The five crowns represent the perfected Quintessence ~ gold and light.

C U L M I N A T I O N

27 Philosopher's Stone

Multiplication

∘ *Build on the projects you have completed* ∘ *Share your wisdom with others* ∘ *Transformation can be effortless*

IN THE LABORATORY

The Philosopher's Stone is the child born to the King and Queen. This substance, variously described as a stone, a powder or an elixir, appears at the end of Rubedo, or conjunction. The Philosopher's Stone, sometimes depicted as a young prince, contains an equal balance of masculine and feminine properties in their perfected states. Once it is achieved, it has the power of multiplication, easily facilitating the transmutation of other metals into silver and gold. In its symbol, depicted on the stone and in the picture opposite, the circles represent the unity of matter; the square shows the balance between the four elements; and the triangle represents the three properties of Sulphur, Mercury and Salt, and the three levels of body, mind and spirit. All are combined as one ~ this is the culmination of the work.

FOR YOU

A perfected child has appeared, playful, full of potential and wise beyond its years. The achievement of this phase signals a new beginning in your life. Combining the best qualities of body, mind and spirit, this androgynous child can unlock the wisdom of the ages. Building on what you have learned, new projects can be initiated and nurtured in an atmosphere of childlike joy and simplicity. You have great power now to transform your situation, using less effort than in the past as a result of the knowledge you have gained from experience. You can bring about great change by sharing this wisdom with others. The Philosopher's Stone brings awareness of the perfection you have always held inside. Joy now reigns as you attain your goals with ease. Share your joy with those around you, bringing new light to their lives.

*The Sun and the Moon are equal partners in the creation of the
Philosopher's Stone, which contains masculine and feminine aspects in
balanced perfection.*

C U L M I N A T I O N

28 Ouroboros

Return

∘ Old patterns return ∘ A new cycle begins ∘ Do not be your own
worst enemy

IN THE LABORATORY

The Ouroboros is a dragon biting its own tail, symbolizing the cyclic aspects of the
work. The Stone of the Philosopher (Primal Matter) and the Philosopher's Stone
are one, differing only in the degree of their perfection. In the alchemical work,
operations are repeated often. The alchemist can make miscalculations and must
then begin again, and through this process of trial and error acquires knowledge.
This process is like the cycle of nature: the miraculous rebirth of the spring leads to
the maturity of summer and the abundant harvest of autumn. Seeds fall to the
Earth as winter's cold grip brings the necessary hibernation before the warmth of
spring causes new life to begin again. As day follows night, hope follows disappointment. These cycles are all part of the cosmic plan.

FOR YOU

The alchemical process is a never-ending spiral, often returning to a similar point,
seen from a higher level. As Primal Matter contains all that is necessary for the production of the Philosopher's Stone, know that wherever you are in the process you
are capable of achieving perfection. Yet, just as the dragon is devouring its own tail,
you may be your own worst enemy. Even after significant gains, you may find yourself dealing with identical issues that challenged you in the past. You are here to
learn these lessons: know that your past experiences have given you the necessary
wisdom to cope with whatever life holds in store for the future. Be one with the flow
of life, and trust that the inevitable changes, set-backs and new challenges you
encounter are part of the great cosmic cycle of the Universe.

[76]

The circle formed by the Ouroboros dragon represents the unity of the alchemical work. At any stage in the process, you may find yourself facing a situation you have faced before. Remember ~ you have everything you need at the start. A new cycle is always beginning.

In the background Oedipus solves the Sphinx's riddle. Likewise, the alchemist solves the riddles of nature, guided here by the god Mercury.

-- PART TWO --

YOUR LABORATORY PROCEDURES

*ALCHEMY IS A TOOL FOR SELF-TRANSFORMATION. IN THE LABORATORY,
the alchemist carefully observes the vessel and the changes occurring within it. An accurate
interpretation of the progression of the work is crucial and serves as a gauge of the alchemist's
increasing knowledge and practical skills. Through trial and error, alchemy's deeper wisdom is
gradually revealed. These successes and failures of experiments mirror the triumphs and
disappointments of daily life. As a substitute for the physical reality of the alchemical laboratory,
the techniques you will employ here are adapted from ancient traditions of divination,
using symbols selected unseen and seemingly at random to reflect the Self.*

Reading the Alchemy Stones

FIVE different readings, consisting of one, two, three, four and seven stones, are
described in this section. Based on alchemical symbolism, they duplicate basic laboratory procedures and embody principles of the work's evolution. Read through them carefully and choose which is most suitable for your situation and area of enquiry. You may
find that a single-stone reading is the easiest way to begin and, as you become more comfortable with this process, you can progress to the more complex readings.

When asking for insights, it will help your concentration to create a time and place of
quiet contemplation, where hectic daily activities can be put aside for the moment. Alchemy affects the body, mind and spirit, so taking a moment to get in touch with each of these
aspects of yourself will deepen the experience. You may want to light a candle and begin
breathing peacefully and consciously. Turn your attention to your body and observe what
you find within. Release any tensions and physical blockages so that your relaxation
increases. On the mental level, observe the thoughts running through your mind. Put aside
any extraneous worries and clear your mind of all preoccupations as you focus on your
question. Then listen to your heart. Ask that you will be able to interpret any message you
receive in a way that will best promote your higher spiritual development.

To read the alchemy stones, first place them in the pouch. Select one or more stones
from the pouch, depending on the layout, and place them in the pattern described. Using
the index *(see pages 94~5)*, find the pages that describe the symbols you have selected. Take
time to read and reflect on each message you receive, asking yourself how it might be

applied to the question you posed. Unlike the symbols of the I-Ching, the Tarot and many of the Runes, there are no reverse meanings for stones that may appear upside down when pulled from the pouch. However, you will find that many of these messages contain seem-ingly contradictory statements that must be carefully weighed and considered.

After reading the meaning of each stone, read the description of its placement position according to the layout you have followed. To integrate these meanings, imagine that you are creating an alloy. Copper and tin combine to form bronze, and both are strengthened by their union. The message of the stone, combined with the meaning of its placement in the layout, will strengthen its relevance to your question. This will be a challenging but rewarding process, and your interpretative skills will sharpen over time. Soon you will develop an intuitive feeling of whether the message received applies directly to the specific question you asked, or to another situation facing you at the moment, or to more universal issues in your life. As you practise, you will learn to gauge the intensity of a message. Some messages will seem right on target, while others will seem only partially applicable. You may even find a message inappropriate and decide to discard it altogether and begin again. Perhaps the way you phrased your question was unsuitable ~ try putting it a different way.

Once you feel comfortable reading the stones for yourself, you may want to do readings for other people. In my own experience, readings work best as a dialogue or conversation in which two people discuss and weigh the possible interpretations of each stone and its position within a layout. Ask the person to feel any physical and emotional responses, to observe whatever mental thoughts arise, and to imagine the spiritual benefits of all potential paths suggested by the reading. Work together to reach a conclusion. At the end of any reading, it is always helpful to record your responses in a journal. This exercise will bring even greater clarity as you begin to express your thoughts and feelings on paper.

As you weigh these messages, remember to apply one of the central axioms of the alchemical process, *Solve et Coagula,* 'dissolve and coagulate'. Decide what you should dis-card and what you should join with and use as guidance in your life. Balance the message of the text with your inner feelings, always bringing your thoughts back to the Self as you seek to apply these stones to your situation. After all, you are the alchemist.

The resurrected
Sun brings

illumination to
the alchemist.

SINGLE/STONE READING

[This reading is best for simple, direct questions about a situation
that you want to transform.]

*The Philosopher's Stone is the child who
appears in the Alembic vessel. Rings of fire
show the transformational power that it
embodies.*

1 ∘ *The Philosopher's Stone*

IN THE LABORATORY

The number one symbolizes the unity of matter and the cyclic nature of the work from
beginning to end. The Stone of the Philosopher (Primal Matter) and the Philosopher's
Stone are one and the same, differing only in the degree of perfection. The alchemist
begins with a single substance, Primal Matter, and proceeds to find the miraculous perfection contained within. Finding this substance at the beginning, you will have everything
you need to bring the work to completion.

FOR YOU

By selecting a single stone, you can illuminate any question you want to ask. Pose your
query in a simple, straightforward manner, keeping the issues focused on a single point.

The stone may not give a specific answer; more likely it will suggest ways you can interpret your situation. Thus, the phrasing of your question should remain open. For example, you might ask, 'What attitude should I adopt to bring the best results to this situation?' or perhaps, 'What would be my next step to initiate a process of positive change?' Read carefully the passage that describes the meaning of the stone you have chosen. Take some time to reflect upon the message you receive, as the answer you seek is already contained within you. The simplicity of a single stone can, on reflection, offer multiple interpretations for you to consider. Insight will come through this process of interpretation.

After reflecting on the stone you have pulled, another question may arise. You can continue your query by pulling another stone in the same manner as the first. In this way, you can create a series of stepping-stones, pulling a single stone at a time. Close your session when you feel completion.

SAMPLE READING

1 ° The Philosopher's Stone

Rubedo

ON one of her walks, Marie finds a beautiful antique stone that may have been part of a pendant. It reminds her of a dream she had many years ago in which she gave a small piece of healing jade to a wounded man. Because she is so struck by this object, she asks about its significance in her life.

Pulling Rubedo, she first observes the remarkable similarity between the symbol on this stone, two lines forming a single straight shape, and the straight slender form of the object she has found. In Rubedo, the King and Queen make passionate love and conceive a child, the Philosopher's Stone. Its message is one of unity, when plans take shape and come to life.

SUMMARY: Marie feels that her antique stone symbolizes the integration she has achieved within, the healing of the wounded man joining with her feminine self. She also has been working for several years on a plan that is now coming to life. As in Rubedo ~ when the Philosopher's Stone takes form ~ the small stone Marie has found becomes her own Philosopher's Stone, signifying the completion of her project. This reading is a good example of how something observed in nature, or a found object, can have an alchemical meaning.

TWO⁄STONE READING

[This reading is best for weighing up issues that keep recurring over a long period of time.]

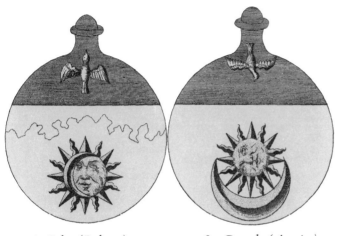

The Sun and the Moon must be separated and joined within the Alembic vessel. Gases, represented by the rising and falling birds, evaporate above and return below as condensation.

1 ◦ Solve (Release)   *2 ◦ Coagula (Acquire)*

IN THE LABORATORY

Two is the number of duality. A central axiom of alchemy is *Solve et Coagula*, 'dissolve and coagulate', let go and bring together ~ release and acquire. As the Sun and the Moon dance around each other in the Alembic vessel, small birds rise and fall, representing the liquids and gases that are being constantly distilled, evaporated and condensed. During these repetitions, fixed matter becomes volatile and volatile matter is fixed; that is, solids transform into liquids and liquids become solid. Throughout these continuous fluctua⁄ tions, the impurities of Primal Matter and its two principal properties, the masculine Philosophic Sulphur and the feminine Philosophic Mercury, are removed and the refined essences of the Sun and the Moon begin to emerge.

FOR YOU

Like the ascending and descending birds, lift your heart to receive advice towards achiev⁄ ing a positive outcome. Aspire to your highest goals. At the same time, delve deep inside and ask if your desires resonate with the truest essence of your inner self.

In selecting two stones, place them side by side. As you read the message of the stone on the left, ask yourself how that message might help you to release the outmoded aspects of your life that are hindering your progress to your desired goal. As you reflect on the message of the stone on the right, select those aspects of its meaning that will help you acquire the resources you need now to bring positive aspects to your life. The two positions can also be thought of as the 'past' and the 'present', helping you to let go of persistent recurring problems and to acquire new strengths.

SAMPLE READING

1° Solve
(Release)
Adept

2° Coagula
(Acquire)
Quintessence

SEVERAL years ago, Anne went through an acrimonious divorce. Soon she will have to face her ex-husband, and his new wife, at their daughter's graduation. She asks how she can best prepare herself for this, and pulls Adept and Quintessence.

Her reading is aided by reflecting on the alchemical images with each stone. At first, it seems odd that the Adept, a very positive stone, is placed in the position of the past with things that must be released: this stone represents the skilled alchemist uniting the King and Queen in their Chemical Wedding. To Anne, it symbolizes her idea of marriage and the disappointment she felt when her own dissolved. Like the Adept, she must learn control and put this past relationship into perspective.

The message of the Quintessence is one of balance, harmony and equilibrium. Bringing all of her considerable forces together, she can shine forth at her daughter's graduation. Looking at the image of Quintessence (*see page 49*), she can interpret the young woman with the starry halo as her beautiful, talented daughter. Both she and her ex-husband can celebrate her day of triumph.

SUMMARY: Although some emotional residue still exists with this past relationship, Anne realizes that a great deal of healing has occurred. She can enjoy her daughter's special day with a sense of peace, equilibrium and personal accomplishment.

THREE-STONE READING

[This reading provides an intensive exploration of the Self, deepening the answer to your chosen query.]

3 ∘ Spirit

2 ∘ Mind

1 ∘ Body

Below, a man and woman tend the Alembic vessel inside the Athanor furnace. Two angels hold a vessel in which the Roman god Neptune guards the young Apollo and Diana ~ the Sun and Moon deities. The Sun observes from the cosmos above.

IN THE LABORATORY

The number three represents the various trinities found throughout the alchemical work. Philosophic Sulphur and Philosophic Mercury, the masculine and feminine principles, are united in the presence of a third substance, the catalyst Salt. At every stage, the alchemical work progresses simultaneously on three levels ~ the Body, the Mind and the Spirit.

The realm of the Body refers to the physical plane, specifically to operations in the lab-oratory that transform lead into gold. This work takes physical effort ~ pulverizing, sift-ing, washing and heating the substance in the vessel. Primal Matter is purified, and each of the seven metals are perfected through successive stages of heating and cooling, evaporation and condensation, while the alchemist carefully observes and monitors physical changes in the Alembic vessel.

Transformation on the mental plane occurs in the Mind of the alchemist who gains insights about the Self as a result of engaging in the work. Solving alchemy's riddles takes mental effort ~ reading, thinking and thoroughly engaging the Mind. Through study and reflection, the alchemist begins to decipher the symbols and paradoxes of the work, seeing them as a mirror of both conscious and unconscious mental processes. Successes and fail-ures alike are lessons that strengthen the mind and its capacity for understanding.

Spiritual transformation is the highest level, engaging both the Spirit and the heart. As metals are transmuted from lead into gold, the alchemist begins to understand cosmic con-nections that exist between physical, mental and spiritual realms. Alchemy is a spiritual path that can reveal the most profound mysteries of the Universe. The creation of gold from lead duplicates the creation of the world and its perfection from initial chaos. The alchemist achieves spiritual enlightenment by connecting the Self (which is the micro-cosm) to the greater Universe (or macrocosm). The Divine can be experienced by touch-ing the higher Self within and perceiving Oneness, unity and unconditional love.

FOR YOU

For this layout, select three stones and place them in a vertical row, with the first stone (Body) at the bottom, the second stone (Mind) in the middle, and the third stone (Spirit) on top. As you look at these three stones, balance their messages with their placement in this spread, specifically their connections to Body, Mind and Spirit.

The stone on the bottom represents the physical plane or the material level of the work. Ask yourself how this message can be carried out in the real world. What are the practical applications of this message to your question? How can it nourish your physical and mate-rial needs? The stone in the middle position represents the mental or intellectual plane. Being aware of both conscious and unconscious desires, weigh and balance its advice. What can you learn from this stone that will enhance your mental attitude in viewing your situation? The highest stone relates to the spiritual aspects of your question. Reflect on its message in the light of your own spiritual path. How can this message help you achieve what you desire, and at the same time reflect your oneness with cosmic order?

[86]

SAMPLE READING

3 ° Spirit
Initiate

2 ° Mind
Philosopher's
Stone

1 ° Body
Earth

MICHAEL asks whether he should move home. He now lives in the country some distance from his workplace and would prefer a shorter commute; however, he is concerned about the higher cost of a new home nearer the city. He draws Earth, Philosopher's Stone and then Initiate.

The Earth, in the position of the Body or physical plane, underscores the practical aspects of his question and relates to the land and to the importance of establishing permanent roots. Earth suggests the fixed grounding of a home to nurture his physical well-being, while at the same time he is reminded of the volatile nature of his continual travel with its associated stress. It also urges him to consider carefully the financial impact of his move.

The Philosopher's Stone at the Mind level is a powerful combination with great impact. It could symbolize a new beginning from which fresh projects could be initiated and nurtured. The geometric symbols within this stone represent unity, stability and growth. Michael must weigh his potential move against each of these three goals. The power of multiplication within this stone may refer to his increasing mental powers, and to the ease with which he will promote new projects.

The Initiate at the level of the Spirit reveals a new moon, a new cycle and a guide, perhaps from within, to a new direction. Intuition and unconscious urges are the foundation of this potential transformation, unifying the Self and the Spirit at a higher level. This stone also signals the importance of nature to Michael's Spirit and the loss he might feel when he moves back to the city, yet it suggests the initiation of a spiritual quest, or another new path in his life.

SUMMARY: This is a positive reading, which endorses Michael's desire to move while recognizing his need to feel grounded. A move will heighten mental integration and promote the genesis of many new projects. The level of the Spirit suggests an exciting new direction for Michael's energies; however, he may also experience some longing for the quiet beauty of the countryside.

FOUR⁄STONE READING

[This reading works best for finding stability and for setting new goals.
It addresses issues of material possessions, emotions, thoughts and energy.]

Four women stand on symbols of the four elements ~ Earth, Water, Air and Fire. In alchemy, all matter is composed of these. In the vessels above are the stages of the work ruled by each element.

1 ◦ Earth   2 ◦ Water   3 ◦ Air   4 ◦ Fire

IN THE LABORATORY

The alchemist begins the work with raw matter found in the Earth. Water is used to purify the substance through repeated washings. Air represents the rising and falling gases that transform the substance further when heated over a gentle Fire. Through this process the King and Queen are joined, and their child, the Philosopher's Stone, is created.

FOR YOU

Select four stones and place them in a horizontal row from left to right. The first stone on the left is in the position of the Earth, the element governing wealth, material possessions and practical matters. The second position is ruled by the element Water, the realm of love and emotions. The third is Air, the element that oversees mental activities, the world of ideas and anxieties. The fourth is Fire, the element of action, energy and enterprise. Each position combines the symbolism of the four elements within the laboratory.

[88]

Balance the meaning of your four stones with their positions within the layout. The first stone will speak of practical matters and material needs. Ask yourself how the message of the stone might help you find what you seek in the real world. The second stone's message will affect you in the areas of love and emotions in your life. How can this message also clarify your situation and remove impediments? The third stone relates both to your thoughts and anxieties. How can its advice best be used to transform the situation and bring new insights? The fourth stone concerns any new projects you may wish to begin. What parts of this message can help you pursue your desired goals energetically?

SAMPLE READING

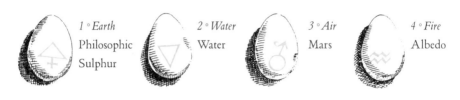

1 ° Earth
Philosophic
Sulphur

2 ° Water
Water

3 ° Air
Mars

4 ° Fire
Albedo

KATE is moving in with her new lover, leaving her home of many years. She asks what she needs to know about this transition and how to avoid mistakes made in past relationships. She draws Philosophic Sulphur, Water, Mars and Albedo.

Philosophic Sulphur highlights many masculine elements in Kate's nature. It calls for refinement, so she should temper her need to control her environment, especially as she enters an established household. The activity of this stone indicates that she is ready to move from her home 'soil' without regrets, to set down new roots. Water in the Water position is doubly powerful, signifying the emotions wrapped up in the transition, both with the new relationship and with those left in the past. Mars is the planet of decisive action. Placed in the realm of Air, of mental activity and transition, it urges her organize herself for the move. Finally, the watery Albedo is placed in the Fire position: rather than reading this as water quenching the transformational energy, she sees it as producing a lot of steam to charge ahead.

SUMMARY: This reading shows an interesting contrast between forces of decisive action and the emotional fluidity of Water and Albedo. Kate can balance her energetic movement forward with a clear recognition of deep, emotional feelings within.

SEVEN-STONE READING

[
This layout is the full cycle, duplicating the complete progression of the
alchemical work to obtain a 'golden' solution. It is best for questions of major life
transitions and for initiating new projects.
]

4 ◦ Refine
(Self)

3 ◦ Transform
(Transition)

5 ◦ Join
(Environment)

2 ◦ Separate
(Past)

6 ◦ Reflect
(Hopes and
Fears)

1 ◦ Find
(Basis)

7 ◦ Aspire
(Outcome)

An Adept explains alchemy to an Initiate. Alchemy is a tree whose roots
grow deep into the earth. Four elements, seven planets and seven
alchemical operations are all symbolized here.

IN THE LABORATORY

The image opposite shows an elder Adept explaining alchemy to a young Initiate. They stand on either side of a tree that contains the Sun, Moon and five stars to symbolize the seven ancient planets that govern the seven metals from lead to gold. At the lower edges are the four elements and their symbols ~ Earth (a lion), Water (a fish), Air (a bird) and Fire (a dragon). The Sun King is refined from fiery Earth, while the Moon Queen emerges from volatile moisture. The seven circles surrounding the tree describe important stages of the work, represented by descending and ascending birds, a unicorn, and a young child arising from the Earth.

The arc of seven alchemy stones is an elaborate layout, duplicating on a small scale the full progression of the alchemical work. Each of the seven positions in this layout represents a stage in the alchemical task which has been reinterpreted to carry a meaning related to the timely progression of your question and its outcome.

FOR YOU

For this reading pull seven stones and place each one in position along an arc as indicated in the picture opposite, beginning in the bottom left-hand corner and ending in the bottom right. As you consider the message of each stone, fuse the meaning of its position with its associated laboratory operation as described below.

Beginning with the first stone, an influential situation or issue is the basis or foundation of this entire reading. This message indicates where you are at the present moment. Just as the alchemist must Find Primal Matter to begin the work, how can this message help you Find the resources that will enable you reach your goal?

The second stone concerns significant events of the past, or a situation that may have recently passed out of your life. To begin the work, Primal Matter must be destroyed in the Alembic vessel. Likewise, how can this message help you Separate and eliminate patterns in your life that are no longer of use to you?

The third stone offers the key for making the transition into your immediate future. Reflect on how this message can help you Transform your situation and make the necessary changes to achieve your goal.

The fourth stone is intimately tied to the Self. As Primal Matter is cleansed through repeated washings in the vessel, how can this message help you Refine and perfect yourself to further the goal of your own self-growth?

The fifth stone points to important people or situations now active within your environment. It signifies the laboratory operations of fusion. How can you use the fifth stone's message to Join with these external forces, improving the situation as well as tap-ping your own internal strengths and wisdom?

The sixth stone signifies both the hopes and fears that you will encounter as you strive to reach your goal. Reflect deeply on its message. Enlighten the awareness of your conscious and unconscious mind.

Finally, the seventh stone may predict an outcome, or it may indicate that a new alchemical cycle is about to begin. In either case, it will offer some additional insights into those higher goals to which you Aspire.

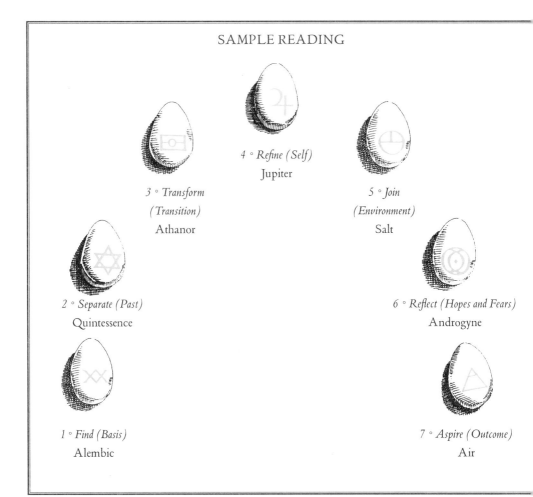

SAMPLE READING

4 ° Refine (Self)
Jupiter

3 ° Transform
(Transition)
Athanor

5 ° Join
(Environment)
Salt

2 ° Separate (Past)
Quintessence

6 ° Reflect (Hopes and Fears)
Androgyne

1 ° Find (Basis)
Alembic

7 ° Aspire (Outcome)
Air

This seven-stone reading is the most challenging of the five layouts described here, requiring you carefully to balance and weigh the message of each stone with the meaning of its position. The sequencing of these seven positions may remind you of a Tarot reading, but the number seven is also a very powerful alchemical number, being the sum of the three alchemical principles and the four elements. Throughout the alchemical process, each of the seven metals, ruled by the seven planets, must be refined before reaching its full potential. This layout thus represents a summation of the alchemical work, a re-creation of the laboratory process from beginning to end.

PETER has been offered a new job. While he is inclined to accept this position, he wonders what impact it will have on the direction of his life.

The first stone, the basis of this reading, is the Alembic, the vessel in which the alchemical work transpires. This stone suggests that Peter has set the forces in motion to bring a new chapter of his life into being. Quintessence, a stone of balance and equilibrium, is in the position of Separate. This represents the past ~ perhaps there will be some disruption in his life as changes occur and some of the balance of his present life begins to dissolve. The stone of transition calls for increasing energy and activity, as he has pulled the Athanor furnace, a stone in which heat is applied to the project at hand. Jupiter is found in the position of the Self, which promises to bring him wealth, abundance and new wisdom. Salt is in the Environment position, indicating that Peter, or someone around him, will serve as an important catalyst for bringing all these new changes about. The sixth stone, in the Hopes and Fears position, is a most interesting choice, for he has drawn one of the powerful culminating stones, the Androgyne. In following this new path, Peter hopes to achieve a new union and oneness within, perhaps also to meet new people and join with them. His fears manifest as the flip side of this stone, that he will miss some of the independence and individuality he enjoys in his present job. Finally, in the position of Aspire, or outcome, is the element, Air. This stone indicates that much new mental activity will be sparked by this new position. He will have a great deal of mobility and his influence will be far-reaching.

SUMMARY: In general, this reading promises abundance, energy and growth if Peter accepts the new position. He should be aware, however, that his life is expanding and that some disruptive changes are to be expected in the transition.

KEY TO THE ALCHEMY STONES

THE rounded shape of the twenty-eight alchemy stones shown here duplicates the interior of the alchemist's flask in which the golden symbol of each ingredient magically appears. These symbols are derived from those found in traditional alchemical manuscripts and must be deciphered by every alchemist in order to complete the work.

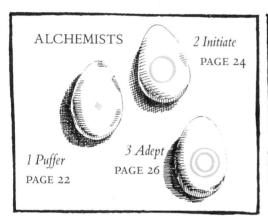

ALCHEMISTS

2 Initiate
PAGE 24

3 Adept
PAGE 26

1 Puffer
PAGE 22

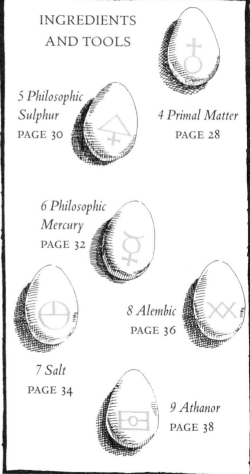

INGREDIENTS
AND TOOLS

*5 Philosophic
Sulphur*
PAGE 30

4 Primal Matter
PAGE 28

*6 Philosophic
Mercury*
PAGE 32

8 Alembic
PAGE 36

7 Salt
PAGE 34

9 Athanor
PAGE 38

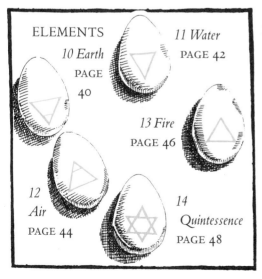

ELEMENTS

10 Earth
PAGE 40

11 Water
PAGE 42

13 Fire
PAGE 46

12 Air
PAGE 44

14 Quintessence
PAGE 48

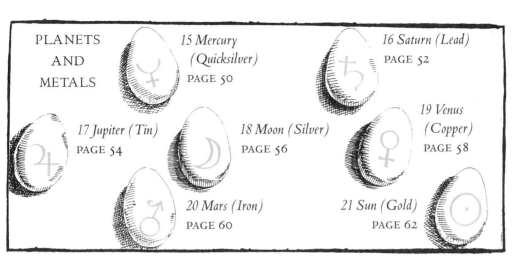

PLANETS AND METALS

15 Mercury (Quicksilver)
PAGE 50

16 Saturn (Lead)
PAGE 52

17 Jupiter (Tin)
PAGE 54

18 Moon (Silver)
PAGE 56

19 Venus (Copper)
PAGE 58

20 Mars (Iron)
PAGE 60

21 Sun (Gold)
PAGE 62

STAGES OF COMPLETION

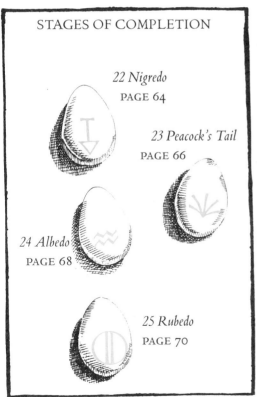

22 Nigredo
PAGE 64

23 Peacock's Tail
PAGE 66

24 Albedo
PAGE 68

25 Rubedo
PAGE 70

CULMINATION

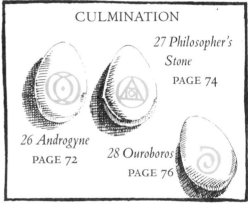

27 Philosopher's Stone
PAGE 74

26 Androgyne
PAGE 72

28 Ouroboros
PAGE 76

HOW TO USE THIS INDEX

Match the symbol of the alchemy stone in your reading with one of these shown here. Look up the page in the book to find an explanation of its role in the laboratory, together with suggestions as to how to adapt its message to your question. You will also find an alchemical illustration for further illumination and insight.

FURTHER READING

Burckhardt, Titus. *Alchemy.* Longmead, England: Element Books, 1987

Coudert, Allison. *Alchemy: The Philosopher's Stone.* London: Wildwood House, 1980

The Emerald Tablet of Hermes. Translations and commentary compiled by Jon Marshall on the web site: http://www.levity.com.alchemy.html

Fabricius, Johannes. *Alchemy: The Medieval Alchemists and their Royal Art.* London: Diamond Books, 1989

Gilchrist, Cherry. *The Elements of Alchemy.* Rockport, Massachusetts: Element Books, 1991

Holmyard, E. J. *Alchemy.* 1957. Reprint. New York: Dover, 1990; London: Dover, 1991

Klossowski de Rola, Stanislas. *Alchemy: The Secret Art.* New York: Avon Books, 1973; London: Thames and Hudson, 1992

———. *The Golden Game: Alchemical Engravings of the Seventeenth Century.* New York: George Braziller, 1988; London: Thames and Hudson, 1988

McLean, Adam. *The Alchemical Mandala.* Grand Rapids, Michigan: Phanes Press, 1990

Pearson, Carol. *Awakening the Heroes Within.* San Francisco: Harper San Francisco, 1991

River, Lindsay and Sally Gillespie. *The Knot of Time: Astrology and the Female Experience.* New York: Harper and Row, 1987; London: Women's Press, 1987

Roberts, Gareth. *The Mirror of Alchemy.* Toronto: University of Toronto Press, 1994; London: British Library, 1994

Silberer, Dr. Herbert. *Problems of Mysticism and its Symbolism.* Translated by Dr. Smith Ely Jelliffe. 1917. Reprint. New York: Samuel Weiser, 1970

Thompson, C. J. S. *The Lure and Romance of Alchemy.* Wiltshire: R. Beard, 1994

ACKNOWLEDGEMENTS

This book has grown through the shared wisdom of many friends and colleagues. Janet Saad-Cook brought the Light through her art, and her wisdom and understanding of the Tarot and Astrology. Deep appreciation goes to Josephine Withers and Carol Pearson for founding a women's spirituality group, where I explored ritual magic and other spiritual paths. In the company of the Moon Sisters ~ Jeanne, Sally, Leslie, Mary, Lori Gene, Neener, Nicole and Helen ~ I learned that nature and the river can teach most of the lessons one needs to know. The Loose Canon ~ Mary Ann, Margaret, Abbey, Paula, Diana, Sieglinde, Diane, Susan, Eleanor, Deborah and Sarah ~ helped me keep my sense of humour within the academic community. From Milton Trager and the Trager family, I discovered the gentle, effortless ways to produce profound change. Janet Nolan's life of personal transformation has been an inspiration, and her art reveals the availability and beauty of primal matter in the everyday world. Johanna Mitchell provided astrological insights and encouragement. The Special Collections staff at the Glasgow University Library have graciously aided my study of original alchemical manu-scripts and printed books. Janet Saad-Cook, Janet Nolan, Jeanne Hoyle, Margaret Whitt, Carol Pearson, Johanna Mitchell, Anne Lanctot, Jennifer Thurston, Amanda and Nicole Cook gave many useful suggestions to finalize the manuscript bring it into form.

PICTURE CREDITS

Images on pages 2, 15, 20, 39, 77 with permission of the Special Collections Department, Glasgow University Library, Scotland. All other images courtesy of *Alchemy* by Johannes Fabricius published by HarperCollins.

EDDISON · SADD EDITIONS

Editor	Sophie Bevan
Proofreader	Nikky Twyman
Senior Art Editor	Sarah Howerd
Illustrator	Richard Earley
Picture Researcher	Liz Eddison
Production	Hazel Kirkman
	and Charles James